take a **closer** look

for teens

take a closer look

for teens

*Uncommon and Unexpected Insights That Are Real,
Relevant, and Ready to Change Your Life*

Jonathan Rogers

HOWARD BOOKS
A DIVISION OF SIMON & SCHUSTER
New York   London   Toronto   Sydney

Our purpose at Howard Books is to:
· *Increase faith* in the hearts of growing Christians
· *Inspire holiness* in the lives of believers
· *Instill hope* in the hearts of struggling people everywhere
Because He's coming again!

HOWARD
BOOKS

Published by Howard Books, a division of Simon & Schuster, Inc.
1230 Avenue of the Americas, New York, NY 10020
www.howardpublishing.com

Take a Closer Look for Teens © 2007 by GRQ, Inc.

ISBN-13: 978-1-4165-4214-8
ISBN-10:   1-4165-4214-0
ISBN 13: 978-1-58229-685-2 (gift edition)
ISBN 10:   1-58229-685-5 (gift edition)

10 9 8 7 6 5 4 3 2 1

HOWARD and colophon are registered trademarks of Simon & Schuster, Inc.
Manufactured in the United States of America

For information regarding special discounts for bulk purchases, please contact: Simon & Schuster Special Sales at 1-800-456-6798 or business@simonandschuster.com.

Managing Editor: Lila Empson
Associate Editor: Chrys Howard
Design: Whisner Design Group

I have called you by name, you are mine.

Isaiah 43:1 ESV

Contents

Introduction

Have you ever noticed that sometimes the more you look at something, the less you see it? You take the same route to school every day, but you rarely pay much attention to the things you see out the window. You know the way like you know the back of your hand, but in a way you don't know it at all. You pass right by things that would really jump out at someone seeing them for the first time—the misspelling on a street sign, the goofy yard art on a neighbor's lawn, the little sun-dappled stream you cross on the way.

Sometimes the same thing happens with Scripture. You've seen a story or a passage so many times that you stop paying attention. "Our Father, who art in heaven . . ." "The Lord is my shepherd . . ." "For God so loved the world . . ." You know those passages, you love them, but maybe you've stopped expecting much from them. The purpose of this book is to stop you on the familiar paths of the Bible and say, "Have you ever noticed this?" "Look at this little detail . . ." "Bet you've never thought of it this way . . ." When you take a closer look at Scripture, you always see things you've never seen before. After all, it's the word of God. It ought to be rich and deep and multifaceted. It ought to contain things you've never noticed before, no matter how many times you've looked.

If you want to get the most out of this book, you're going to have to open your mind and your heart. This book asks you to read in a different way. Resist the urge to skim past the familiar. Slow down. Enjoy the scenery, even when you think you've seen it a hundred times before. There's a lot to see here!

Call to Me, and I will answer you,
and show you great and mighty
things, which you do not know.

Jeremiah 33:3 NKJV

Jacques-Yves Cousteau

Sometimes we are lucky enough to know that our lives have been changed, to discard the old, embrace the new, and run head-long down an immutable course.

Look, I am about to do something new.

Isaiah 43:19 HCSB

No Double Standards

When morning came, there was Leah! So Jacob said to Laban, "What is this you have done to me? I served you for Rachel, didn't I? Why have you deceived me?"

Laban replied, "It is not our custom here to give the younger daughter in marriage before the older one."

Genesis 29:25–26 NIV

The Big Picture

Jacob was used to getting his own way. He was used to doing whatever it took to get it. Before he was even born, when his mother was told she was carrying twins, God said the older son would serve the younger. In those days, in that part of the world, age meant rank and rank meant everything, so this was a weird prophecy. But it came true. Jacob's name in Hebrew even means "deceiver." Jacob once cheated his older brother Esau out of the majority of his inheritance by bribing him with a bowl of soup. He once dressed in Esau's clothes and wrapped himself in animal skins in order to trick his old, blind father into giving him the blessing that belonged to his older brother. Jacob seemed to be winning, but by that time Esau was murderously angry and fed up with his brother's tricks. Jacob had to run for his life.

Jacob ran to Haran, where his mother had family. He ended up living with his uncle Laban and working for him. And he fell in love with Laban's younger daughter, Rachel. Laban agreed to let Jacob marry his daughter, but for a price: Jacob had to work for Laban for seven years without pay. At the end of the seven years, Jacob would have his bride. Jacob agreed and put in his seven years of labor. The Bible says the time passed quickly for Jacob because he loved Rachel so much.

Then, at the end of seven years, there was a wedding and a big party. Wedding parties in those days lasted for days and went late into the night. As Jacob was finally ready to spend his first night with his new bride, Laban brought to him a woman beautifully dressed, probably wearing a veil. Little did Jacob know that his bride was not Rachel! Laban pulled the old switcheroo on Jacob. In the morning, Jacob realized that he had married Rachel's older sister Leah! Of course he was surprised and angry, and he con-fronted Laban. Laban had his answer ready: "It is not our custom here to give the younger daughter in marriage before the older one." What could Jacob say? Laban offered to let Jacob marry Rachel for another seven years' work, and Jacob agreed, but their relationship was forever strained.

Good Lord, deliver us . . . from all the deceits of
the world, the flesh, and the devil.
The Book of Common Prayer

After a lifetime of tricking people by breaking the rules, Jacob became easy prey for a man who tricked him by simply sticking to the rules. You can just imagine the look of innocence and mock surprise on Laban's face when he said those words to his disappointed nephew: "It is not our custom here to give the younger daughter in marriage before the older one." Jacob knew it to be true. It wasn't the custom among his people to bless the younger before the older either.

The irony is that it was Jacob's trickery, his tendency to go around the rules that made him susceptible to Laban's trickery. It never occurred to Jacob to wonder why his uncle seemed willing to give him the younger daughter in marriage. Jacob was used to working things so that the younger had an unfair advantage over the older. So why shouldn't his bride marry before her older sister? He played right into the hands of his craftier uncle. Perhaps Jacob had gotten an inflated view of his own cleverness. Perhaps he thought he was helping God fulfill his own prophecies. In any case, the cheater got cheated. The trickster got tricked.

> *Oh, what a tangled web we weave, when first we practice to deceive!*
>
> Sir Walter Scott

You probably know people who get their way by deceiving and breaking all the rules. They tell their parents they're one place when they're really someplace else. They find a way to cheat, then their grades are just as good as the people who actually studied. They use their friends. But people who live that way are more vulnerable than they know. Of course, there's always the possibility that they could get caught by their parents or their teachers or the police. But the real danger is if they don't get caught.

When you get away with enough deceit, you begin to believe that the rules that apply to everybody else don't apply to you. When you place yourself outside the limitations of the rules, you also place yourself outside their protection. Following the rules may seem less exciting than living on the edge, but consider what happened to Jacob: out of the habit of living by his society's standards, he never asked the obvious question: why, Uncle Laban, would you let me marry little sister Rachel while big sister Leah is still single? There's always somebody a little smarter, a little more experienced. And even if there isn't, there's always God watching what you do.

Evil men and impostors will go from bad to worse, deceiving and being deceived.
2 Timothy 3:13 NIV

There is a "first things first" spiritual application to this story that shows that God has a certain order we must do things in, too, as C. H. Spurgeon points out:

"Many men desire the beautiful and well-favored Rachel of joy and peace in believing, but they must first be wedded to the tender-eyed Leah of repentance. Every one falls in love with happiness, and many would cheerfully serve twice seven years to enjoy it, but according to the rule of the Lord's kingdom, the Leah of real holiness must be beloved of our soul before the Rachel of true happiness can be attained."

Just like Jacob did not need to have cheated his brother and father to obtain God's promise, when he is tricked by Laban, hope is not lost. Gerard Van Groningen states:

"The account of Jacob's flight to and experiences with his relatives in Padan Aram demonstrates God's grace and providence. Jacob received assurance that he would inherit the promises given to Abraham, his grand-father, and Isaac, his father, concerning the seed, the land, and the Lord's abiding presence. . . . The Lord prospered Jacob while he served Laban and protected him when he fled back to Canaan, the Promised Land."

Zooming **In**

Bigamy, or having two wives, is a crime according to today's laws, but in the Bible it wasn't unusual for a man to have more wives than one. King Solomon, in fact, had more than three hundred! It was not only common practice, but the Old Testament law *required* that the inheritance given to the oldest son be twice as much as the amount given to any other son. He often also got the right to carry on the family name and may have been the head of not just his own family, but the whole family clan.

It's tempting to cheat to get what you want. Jacob did, even though he inherited the promises of Abraham, and had predictions made about him before he was born. But it caught up with him.

Through the
Eyes of
Your Heart

Is there anything that you love enough that you could imagine working years and years to get it? How would you feel if someone took it away at the last minute?

Have you ever tried to make something happen for yourself, rather than waiting for God to do his thing?

Is there some flaw or problem that you see in someone else that really bugs or annoys you? Is it ever because you know you have the same problem yourself?

The Many Sides of God

Then Moses said, "Now show me your glory." And the LORD said, "I will cause all my goodness to pass in front of you. . . . When my glory passes by, I will put you in a cleft in the rock and cover you with my hand until I have passed by."

Exodus 33:18–19, 22 NIV

The Big Picture

Moses had gotten glimpses of God's glory many times. He saw God's glory in a bush that burned but was not consumed. He saw God's glory in the miracles and plagues leading up to the Israelites' departure from Egypt. He walked across the floor of the Red Sea, the water standing like walls on either side of his path. Those encounters with God's glory and power transformed Moses into a man of courage and a genuine leader.

The people he led, however, were not as courageous or as faithful as Moses. They saw God's glory and marveled at his power, but it wasn't long before they forgot and started thinking like people who had never experienced such an awesome God. One of the first things they did after they walked through the Red Sea was to reject the God who had freed them. When Moses went up a smoke-covered Mount Sinai to meet with God and receive the Ten Commandments, the people gave up on him. While he was gone they turned to idol worship. As soon as they began bowing down to the golden calf, though, Moses reappeared to call them on it. He was furious at the people for their unfaithfulness to God. If this was how they were going to act, he wondered, what did God expect him to do with this bunch?

But God refused to give up on them, even if Moses was ready to. After the golden calf incident, God told Moses that he was going to go ahead with his plans to bring the people into the Promised Land, even though the people were sinful and rebellious. But Moses had questions. He didn't doubt that God could handle the people, but Moses wasn't sure if he could. Made bold by his frustration, Moses asked God to reveal his presence. Moses needed another look at God, one like he had never had before. God agreed to this unusual request. When Moses returned to the mountain to receive the two new tablets with the Ten Commandments, God made a way for Moses to see him in his glory. God said, "I will cause all my goodness to pass in front of you." What God showed him was not the thunder and smoke that Moses expected, but the glory of his goodness.

Before I begin to think and consider the love of God and the mercy and compassion of God, I must start with the holiness of God.

Martin Lloyd-Jones

Moses thought he knew what he was going to need if he was supposed to lead those rebellious Israelites out of the wilderness and into the Promised Land. He thought he needed a good look at God's power. That, Moses believed, would give him the reassurance he needed to carry on. But God knew better. Moses didn't really doubt God's power—how could he after all he had seen? But perhaps, in the midst of all his struggles, he had lost sight of God's goodness. What Moses really needed was a good look at God's goodness. That's what would really motivate him to serve God and love God's people.

God's glory and goodness are both part of who he is. They are two sides, two aspects of the same amazing God. So Moses got both what he wanted and what he needed. He saw not only the wonderful, amazing, supernatural glory of God and his power, but also his goodness, his faithfulness, the very aspects of God's character that would make him keep his promises to Moses. The different sides of God don't contradict each other. Even when he is glorious and powerful beyond what human beings can handle, God is good.

> The glory of Him who moves everything penetrates through the universe. . . .
>
> Dante Alighieri

Why is it that your parents are great when they're doing stuff for you or giving you stuff, but they seem so wrong when they are laying down rules? Why is it that your friends are cool when they agree with you, but idiots when they don't? People are complicated and have different sides; some you like, and some you don't. God is that way too. He doesn't fit into anybody's box. He won't be limited to what anybody thinks he ought to be. Which is to say, you can't pick and choose the things you like about God and ignore or deny the rest.

Apply It
to Your Life

God is who he is, and if people are complicated, God is more complicated. You can't just take him when it's easy to see he's on your side. You have to take him when he disagrees with you, shows you your faults, your weaknesses, your sins. God is good and glorious, but he is also holy and righteous, and if you would have him, you have to take the whole of him. But remember that he is love, and—like parents and friends—he does what's best for you.

Surely goodness and lovingkindness will follow me all the days of my life.

Psalm 23:6 NASB

Even though God answered Moses' request and showed himself, John MacArthur explains that he didn't reveal all of himself:

"God promises proximity but never full revelation. So God says to Moses, 'I'll tell you what, I'll tuck you in the cleft of a rock and I'll let My—and the Hebrew means—My hind quarters, My back parts.' I like to think of it as afterglow. You can't see the whole deal, but I'll let you see My afterglow."

As A. W. Tozer wrote, God's holiness is well beyond our ability to imagine, and certainly beyond our ability to comprehend:

"We cannot grasp the true meaning of the divine holiness by thinking of someone or something very pure and then raising the concept to the highest degree we are capable of. God's holiness is not simply the best we know infinitely bettered. We know nothing like divine holiness. It stands apart, unique, unapproachable, incomprehensible and unattainable."

Zooming **In**

Different religions have gods from whom their worshipers must hide their faces. In ancient Greece, the Gorgon Medusa was so ugly, with snakes for hair, that a man could not look at her or he would turn to stone. But she was not invincible. Perseus was able to approach her with a mirror reflecting her ugliness and cut off her head.

The Yin-Yang symbol of Chinese Daoism is a circle divided in half. One half is black, the other white. In the black half is a white dot; in the white half is a black dot. The idea is that bad has a little good and good a little bad. Both characteristics are there, but unlike God, neither is pure or perfect.

It is hard, sometimes, to think of God as having a personality. But like people, there are different sides to God's personality, and it takes time to get to know him.

Through the
Eyes of
Your Heart

Do you ever like certain aspects of God better than others? Do you like that he is loving and compassionate, but wish he were not quite so holy or just? List your reasons and think about why.

When you are frustrated and the future is unclear, do you ever wish God would show himself and prove that he will take care of you? What can give you faith when this does not happen?

There are so many sides of God's personality. Moses asked to be able to see God's glory. If you could be shown one part of God's personality, what part would you ask to see? Why?

Bring It to God Yourself

The Big Picture

When you are reading through the complicated religious laws and regulations of Leviticus and Deuteronomy, you might feel tempted to skip ahead to a more interesting part of the Bible. But there are some real treasures to be found amid all those rules. Take the fellowship offering, for example. The fellowship offering, also called the peace offering, was unlike any in the complex system of Old Testament offerings and sacrifices.

The offering of sacrifices was at the center of Old Testament worship. The Israelites kept themselves clean before God by taking something they valued and giving it over to God. The idea of sacrifice had been around for some time—about as long as human beings have been around. The trouble between Cain and Abel began with differing opinions over what was an acceptable sacrifice. Noah offered sacrifices; so did Abraham.

Centuries later, at Mount Sinai, God gave specific rules about how sacrifices were to be offered. He detailed which animals were acceptable and which were not. He described how they were to be butchered and what parts were to be offered. And he listed a number of different sacrifices to be offered by different classes of people and for different reasons. Most of the sacrifices were performed by religious professionals. The people handed their sacrifices over to the priests, who offered them up on the people's behalf.

Burnt offerings, grain offerings, drink offerings, sin offerings—in all of these sacrifices, the offering was burned up or poured out, given utterly to God except for a small portion that the priests were allowed to keep for their own nourishment. Every kind of offering had its own set of rules. And those rules were so detailed that you would need to be a professional to get them right. The complexity of the sacrificial laws was a constant reminder that God is a holy God and not to be taken lightly.

But then, in the middle of all that religious complexity, was the fellowship offering, a gesture of friendship between human beings and their God. This was the one sacrifice that the ordinary people brought with their own hands: no priest stood between them and God. And this sacrifice, alone in the sacrificial system, was the only one in which the people were allowed to eat the sacrificial animal.

All men desire peace, but very few desire those things that make for peace.

Thomas à Kempis

Fellowship with God. That's what a life of faith is all about. The whole sacrificial system of the Old Testament emphasized the difference between the holy perfection of God and the failings of his people. But that wasn't the end of the story. The final offering of the sacrificial cycle was the fellowship offering—a celebration of the fact that all is now well between God and his people. There was no need for a priest to stand in the middle. This offering was all about friendship with God. This one was a party.

When the sacrificial animal had been butchered, the fat was brought to the priest to be burned. This was God's share; the fat of an animal, after all, was considered to be the choicest part. Part of the meat was given to the priests; that was payment due for their service to God and to the people. But the rest of the meat was served to the worshipers. Everyone sat down to a celebration, a joyful time of fellowship with God and with each other. In the rest of the offerings and sacrifices, the people sought God's forgiveness. In the fellowship offering, they *celebrated* God's forgiveness.

> *When you enter the realm of grace, you enter the arena of awareness. You become acutely aware of who you really are but also aware that you are forgiven, accepted, loved, and redeemed. Both sinner and saint, rebel and ambassador.*
>
> Steven James

What is the difference between conviction and just plain guilt? To feel guilty is to feel bad about having done something wrong. No doubt the people of Israel felt guilt when they handed animals over to the priests to be slaughtered because of the people's sins. No doubt you feel bad when you realize that you've done wrong in the eyes of God.

Apply It
to Your Life

So what do you do with that bad feeling? In the end, the point isn't for you to feel bad. The point is for you to turn away from wrong habits and actions and to turn toward God. That's what conviction means—conviction moves you from feelings of guilt to actually getting right with God.

"If we confess our sins, he who is faithful and just will forgive us our sins and cleanse us from all unrighteousness" (1 John 1:9 NRSV). If you are in Christ, you don't have to beat yourself up over the things you have done wrong. It's not your job to punish yourself, and that's not what God expects from you. What God expects—what he desires—is restored fellowship. When you have turned back to God, you are a friend of God. Now that's something worth celebrating.

Present your bodies as a living sacrifice, holy and acceptable to God, which is your spiritual worship.

Romans 12:1 ESV

The fellowship offering is sometimes called a peace offering. Ray Stedman explains the kind of peace that comes from fellowship with God:

"No proper life is possible without peace. I am not referring here to the peace of forgiveness. That will come in the next two offerings: the sin and the trespass offerings. It is not peace with God; it is the peace of God we are talking about here. It is peace not in the sense of hostility ceased but in the sense of emotional stability, of an untroubled heart."

The meal enjoyed as part of the fellowship offering was not only a feast for that day, but looked forward to an even greater celebration, as C. F. Keil points out:

"In consequence of this participation of the priests, the feast, which the offerer of the sacrifice prepared for himself and his family from the rest of the flesh, became a holy covenant meal, a meal of love and joy, which represented domestic fellowship with the Lord, and thus shadowed forth, on the one hand, rejoicing before the Lord, and on the other, the blessedness of eating and drinking in the kingdom of God."

Zooming **In**

The word for the fellowship offering, *shelamim*, is from the same root as the word for "shalom," or "peace." That's why this is often called a peace offering. Literally, the word means "whole" and includes the ideas of health, wholeness, and welfare, as well as peace. It is a rich word and makes you think about the wholeness you receive in salvation. It's sometimes given as thanks for salvation, or as a prayer for salvation.

In the Fellowship Offering the breast and the hind leg, both choice pieces, were given to the priest. As part of the ceremony, the breast portion was "waved." The offering was brought to the priest, who put it back in the person's hands, then put their own hands under it and moved them forward, toward the altar, showing voluntary surrender, and back, as a sign of God returning the good gift to the person who made the offering.

> *The rules for fellowship offerings were rules, but also an invitation, an invitation that you bring yourself to God in worship.*

How are you personally involved when you worship God? What do you bring to him with your own hands?

_____

_____

_____

Is there ever part of yourself that you hold back from God, by pretending he doesn't know about it or by denying or forgetting about it during worship?

_____

_____

_____

_____

How does knowing you can have fellowship with God make you feel? What is life like when you do not have fellowship with God?

_____

_____

_____

_____

You Can't Know God Without Knowing His Word

The LORD called again, "Samuel!" Samuel got up and went to Eli, and said, "Here I am, for you called me." But he said, "I did not call, my son; lie down again." Now Samuel did not yet know the LORD, and the word of the LORD had not yet been revealed to him.

1 Samuel 3:6–7 NRSV

The Big Picture

In the dark of the night, a young boy heard a voice calling his name: "Samuel." It was the voice of God, but the boy didn't recognize it. As the Bible says, "Samuel did not yet know the LORD." He was living in the house of God, being raised by priests of God, and yet "he did not yet know the LORD." Samuel would hear the voice of God many more times over the course of his life. He would grow into one of the great prophets of the Old Testament era.

This wasn't the first miracle ever to happen to Samuel. His very existence was a miracle. He was born in answer to the prayer of Hannah, his mother, who suffered through many childless years. She prayed in the temple in Jerusalem, and she prayed so fervently that Eli, the priest, thought she must have been drunk. Samuel came a year later. When Hannah had weaned him, she brought him to Eli to be raised in the temple. Samuel was her offering of gratitude to the God who had answered her prayer.

Samuel lived during a dark time in the history of Israel. The people had not heard from God in a long time. The priests were corrupt. Eli himself, Samuel's guardian, was no great role model and apparently had no experience raising godly children. His sons worked in the temple, but they were wicked and disobeyed God and took advantage of the people who came to worship. They were so bad that God told Eli he was going to punish him and his family and that Eli's sons would die.

But Samuel would grow up to bring the truth of God to his people. He would anoint Israel's first king, Saul. He would also anoint David, the greatest of all the Old Testament kings. And it all started on that dark night, in the spiritually dark house of Eli, the high priest of a spiritually dark nation. God reached out to a boy who didn't yet know him, and the boy said, "Speak, LORD, for your servant is listening." It was a conversation that would change the world.

Until a man has found God, and been found by God, he begins at no beginning, he works to no end.

H. G. Wells

You would think a boy growing up in the house of the Lord, the tabernacle, would be in a great position to grow in godliness. But not during Eli's era. Perhaps it was an indication of the spiritual climate that Eli mistook Hannah's prayer for drunkenness. Was it really that unusual to see people pouring their hearts out in God's house? The high priest of Israel didn't recognize a heartfelt prayer when he saw one. It makes you wonder what people were doing in the tabernacle in those days.

Ironically, the religious corruption Samuel witnessed growing up could have hardened a young person to the things of God. The men who surrounded him were the worst sort of hypocrites—religious professionals who didn't even believe the religion by which they cynically made their living. If Samuel had been deaf to the word of God, who could blame him? But God spoke to Samuel anyway, and Samuel heard his voice. God had a plan for Samuel, and for all of Israel. In spite of all the junk in Samuel's environment, God made himself heard. And he didn't just make himself heard to Samuel. Through Samuel, the word of God came to all of Israel.

> *What this country needs is a man who knows God other than by hearsay.*
>
> Thomas Carlyle

You've probably heard of the old nature vs. nurture debate. What makes you the person you are? Are you preprogrammed to be a certain way (that's the "nature" side), or are you shaped by your environment (that's the "nurture" side)? As anyone can see, there's truth on both sides of that argument. Some of your traits and characteristics you were just born with, and some you have learned from the people around you. But Samuel's story shows that there's more to it than either nature or nurture. God can reach into any life and speak to that person, change that person.

Maybe you look around at your environment and think you're never going to rise above your circumstances. Maybe you come from an unbelieving family or you are in school or social situations where the pressure to deny your faith seems insurmountable. God can still speak into Your Life. He can overrule your environment, overcome even the most deeply ingrained habits and personality quirks. Anyone looking at Samuel's situation would have thought there was little hope of his growing up to be a godly man. But God spoke, Samuel listened, and Israel was never the same again. Are you listening for God? He has a plan for your life too.

> *My word which goes forth from My mouth . . . will not return to Me empty, without accomplishing what I desire, and without succeeding in the matter for which I sent it.*
>
> Isaiah 55:11 NASB

Ronald F. Youngblood shows how Samuel is changed and becomes more and more like God because he hears his word:

"Samuel's openness to serving God would soon enable him to know the Lord in a way that Eli's sons never did. Although the word of the Lord had not yet been revealed to Samuel, that would take place very soon; and as God continued to speak to Samuel through the years, the Lord's word would so captivate him that it would be virtually indistinguishable from 'Samuel's word.'"

According to Robert J. Morgan, God did not speak much in Samuel's time because the people did not want to hear him:

"The moral and spiritual qualities of that generation had declined, and the times were so evil that God had almost stopped communicating. There were few people fit to be called as prophets, and there were few people who would heed the Word of the Lord. It was a shallow time. It was an age of plunging morals and of spiritual dullness."

Zooming **In**

Samuel was a Nazirite, someone who was singled out as dedicated to God. The rules for Nazirites were that they could not eat grapes or raisins or drink grape juice or wine. And they never cut their hair. Some were Nazirites for a specific period of time, but Samson, Samuel, and John the Baptist were Nazirites for life.

Samuel's name is sometimes translated "heard of God," but a closer translation might be "asked of God." The word also has the meaning of "allow to ask," or "lend," or "give." It is because Hannah knew her son was on loan from God, not hers to keep, that she could return him to God for his service.

The story of Samuel as a boy in the tabernacle is an example of how you can know God and how much you need to listen to him.

Through the
Eyes of
Your Heart

How can you be sure that you know God and don't just know about him? What clues can you take from Samuel before and after God spoke to him?

_____

_____

_____

You may have parents who are close to God, like Hannah. Do you ever hope to get by on your parents' faith, rather than knowing God yourself?

_____

_____

_____

Samuel did not know God at first, but when God revealed himself, he called Samuel by name. What does this tell you about how God knows you?

_____

_____

_____

_____

When God Knows Your Name

Samuel saw Eliab and thought, "Surely the LORD's anointed stands here before the LORD." But the LORD said to Samuel, "Do not consider his appearance or his height, for I have rejected him. The LORD does not look at the things man looks at. Man looks at the outward appearance, but the LORD looks at the heart." Then Jesse called Abinadab and had him pass in front of Samuel. But Samuel said, "The LORD has not chosen this one either." Jesse then had Shammah pass by, but Samuel said, "Nor has the LORD chosen this one." Jesse had seven of his sons pass before Samuel, but Samuel said to him, "The LORD has not chosen these." So he asked Jesse, "Are these all the sons you have?" "There is still the youngest," Jesse answered, "but he is tending the sheep."

1 SAMUEL 16:6–11 NIV

**The
Big Picture**

Saul the son of Kish was anointed by Samuel and crowned as the first king in Israel. He was a big guy and won quite a few military victories. But he disobeyed God. He tried to do things his own way. He even offered sacrifices—which was something only priests were supposed to do—to try to get God's help for an upcoming battle. So God rejected him, and told him so through Samuel. But he continued to reign while God, in his own time, chose his replacement.

When God first spoke to Samuel and told him he was going to anoint another king in Saul's place, Samuel was afraid because of Saul. Saul was a violent man, he was angry with Samuel, and he wasn't likely to give up the throne easily. But God told Samuel to go ahead and go to a man named Jesse in Bethlehem. When he got there, God would show him which of Jesse's sons was to be the next king.

When Jesse's sons were paraded before the prophet, Samuel saw Eliab, the oldest, and was impressed. He was sure this must be the one. But God told him not to be impressed by his outward appearance. This strapping young man wasn't the one. Human beings judge people by what's on the outside, but God looks at the heart. He told Samuel to keep looking. The next two sons, Abinadab and Shammah, were brought before Samuel. God rejected them too. So were four more brothers. It appeared that Samuel was out of options. Had God told him wrong? Had he misunderstood? He turned to Jesse: "Are these all the sons you have?"

"There is still the youngest," Jesse answered, "but he is tending the sheep." Not even the boy's father seems to have considered the possibility that he might have what it takes to be king over the Israelites. As soon as the boy appeared, however, God showed Samuel that this was the one he had come looking for. Samuel anointed him on the spot, right there in front of his father and brothers. And then at last we learn the boy's name. He is David, and from that day the Spirit of the Lord came upon him in power.

It is a wise father that knows his own child.
William Shakespeare

The younger always served the older. That's just how it was in the culture of the ancient Near East. Sure there were exceptions. Jacob ruled over Esau, then his son Joseph ruled over his older brothers. But those exceptions were so remarkable, so unusual, that the Bible offers them up as examples of God's unpredictable way of working his will in the world.

So perhaps Jesse can be forgiven if it never occurred to him to nominate his youngest son—the one who was stuck tending the family sheep—for the position of king of Israel. But God refused to be constrained by tradition. "'For My thoughts are not your thoughts, nor are your ways My ways,' declares the LORD" (Isaiah 55:8 NASB). He delights to do the unexpected.

From this side of biblical history, it's hard to picture David as a minor character. And yet, at the start of his story, David had no name. His own father didn't even think to call him in from his menial job in the sheep pasture when the prophet came looking for a new big shot. In human terms, he was a nobody. But when God looked at David, he saw someone different. He saw what David was destined to become.

> The glory and the nothing
> of a name.
>
> Lord Byron

Sometimes you can see that little squint in a classmate's expression, hear that tiny pause in a person's voice, and you realize, "That person doesn't even know my name." It makes you feel pretty unimportant, pretty insignificant, pretty easy to forget. Maybe you find yourself in situations where people know you only as so-and-so's

son or daughter or so-and-so's brother or sister. You can get the feeling sometimes that people only know what's on the outside.

But God knows you for who you really are. And he knows who you will be. You might not ever fight a giant or rule the nation, but God knew and loved David before he did those things, and he knows and loves you, too. He can see into your heart like he did David's. He sees how you feel about him, but he also sees your hurts and sorrows, your hopes and dreams. You never need to be discouraged. God is good, and he knows you better than you know yourself. The God of the universe knows you by name. He knows how many hairs are on your head. You are important to God, and he will never forget you.

Fear not, for I have redeemed you; I have called you by name, you are mine.

Isaiah 43:1 ESV

God also used the humble work David did when he was young to prepare him to be king, as Robert Alter points out:

"By his sheer youth, he has been excluded from consideration, as a kind of male Cinderella, left to his domestic chores instead of being invited to the party. But the tending of flocks will have a symbolic implication for the future leader of Israel, and, in the Goliath story, it will also prove to have provided him with skills useful in combat."

Not only did God have plans for David, Richard Strauss says he also liked what he saw about David when he called him:

"When the youngest was brought in from keeping his father's sheep, God's spiritual x-ray vision perceived a heart that dearly loved him and longed to please him. . . . David had his moments of spiritual failure, as we all do, but few people in Scripture could rival his wholehearted devotion to God. God saw true devotion while David was still a youth."

Zooming **In**

Adam's son Abel is the first shepherd in the Bible. Abraham, Jacob, Rachel (Jacob's wife), and her family were all shepherds, too. But when the Israelites went to Egypt with Joseph, shepherding got less respectable. The Egyptians hated shepherds, and later in Israel, as farming became more popular, tending sheep became a job for youngest sons and servants.

The name of the village of Bethlehem means "House of Bread." Bethlehem is the traditional site of the grave of Rachel, the wife Jacob loved and mother of Joseph. It is also the setting for the events of the book of Ruth, who was David's great-grandmother. At the time of David there was a garrison of Philistine soldiers there oppressing the Israelites.

You may identify with David as the youngest, least appreciated, the one not even invited to important events. But God knew and loved him and had a plan for him.

On days when you feel no one knows your name, how is the story of David's humble beginnings encouraging?

_____

_____

_____

You are not going to become the next king of Israel, but how does knowing God loves you and knows your heart make you feel?

_____

_____

_____

It may be easier to change your attitude than your circumstances. What can you do to have a heart like David, one that pleases God?

_____

_____

_____

_____

What in the World . . . ?

Behold, I create new heavens and a new earth, and the former things shall not be remembered or come into mind. But be glad and rejoice forever in that which I create; for behold, I create Jerusalem to be a joy, and her people to be a gladness. I will rejoice in Jerusalem and be glad in my people; no more shall be heard in it the sound of weeping and the cry of distress.

Isaiah 65:17–19 ESV

The Big Picture

Even before he began to prophesy, Isaiah was a pretty influential figure in Jerusalem society. He was a temple priest, and he also was well connected with the king and his court. That put him in a great position to carry out the very unpleasant task God had for him: to tell God's chosen people how they had offended God with their stubbornness and sin. This was about 250 years after David, at a time when the power of David and the glory of Solomon had faded and the Jews were struggling just to survive.

Much like today, international politics were extremely complicated in Isaiah's time. Jerusalem seemed constantly to be in the crosshairs of one world power or another—especially the Assyrians, who were the superpower of the day. The people of Judah found it hard to trust in God alone when thousands of Assyrian chariots were poised on their borders. There was always the temptation to forget about God and seek security in political or military alliances instead.

God gave prophecies through Isaiah that he would judge the wicked Assyrians, however—and the Arameans, Philistines, Moabites, Egyptians, Babylonians, and so on. Much of Isaiah's writing is about God's sovereignty over the great political powers of the world. But he speaks to the hearts of his people, too, who would choose the security of political power over a faithful relationship with the God of the universe. Isaiah tells these people that God is going to judge Judah like he judged Israel and that they will be carried off into captivity by the Babylonians.

The second half of Isaiah's book is the good news, though. The good news is that God will not forget his people, that he will bring them back from captivity, that he will restore them. He names Cyrus of Persia as the ruler who will give the order for the captives to return, something like 150 years later.

But Isaiah goes even further. His prophecies include the promise of Jesus, who will be more than a world political leader, but the Savior of all of humanity from their own sinful hearts. He predicts the coming of God's Son, the virgin birth, and Christ's suffering and death. And he foretells the beautiful and perfected world that will come to be when Christ comes again.

The unrest of this weary world is
its unvoiced cry after God.

Theodore T. Munger

Bad breakups. Final exams. Acne. What do those things have to do with the book of Isaiah? They are all results of the Fall. There is brokenness in the world around you. You might shrug your shoulders and say, "That's just the way it is." Maybe it is. But that's not the way it's always going to be. God doesn't intend to leave everything broken. He sent Jesus to restore the relationship between God and people. That process has started and will be completed when Christ returns again. God is also going to restore your relationship to the world around you. You are ultimately going to be like Adam and Eve in the Garden of Eden, walking with God and enjoying everything he has created all around you.

Does that sound like irrelevant religious talk to you? Think about this: if the brokenness of the world is "just the way it is," why can't you get used to the fact that your body gets sick, your friends get mad at you, and your car breaks down? Because this isn't what you were made for. You were made for something much better: a new heaven and a new earth.

According to Isaiah, God is not just going to fix up the current broken world. He is going to re-create it. The idea of a completely new heaven and earth can be scary. Everything familiar would be gone, like going to a new school or moving to a new town. But God promises that he will make it so good you cannot help but be glad and rejoice.

> *Sometimes we are lucky enough to know that our lives have been changed, to discard the old, embrace the new, and run headlong down an immutable course.*
>
> Jacques-Yves Cousteau

You live in a time when "new" is always supposed to be "improved," at least if you can believe
everything advertisers tell you. But you have probably been through some unpleasant changes, too.
There is plenty of change in this life you wish didn't
happen: death, disease, divorce. Sometimes what
you really want might be something stable and
predictable rather than new, whether it promises to be an improvement or
not.

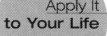

Apply It
to Your Life

There may have even been some changes in your life because of being a
Christian. You might experience difficulty or even persecution for expressing
or living out your faith. You might have lost some old friends. You might have
mixed feelings about God changing things on an even grander scale. Or
maybe your life is not so bad and you would like it to stay that way. But neither your life nor anyone else's is perfect. And God *is* perfect, and he wants
to share his perfection with you. Trust that when God makes all things new,
they will be not only improved, but perfected. And he will be there, the best
friend you could hope for in a new school or new neighborhood.

Do not remember the past events, pay no attention to
things of old. Look, I am about to do something new.
Isaiah 43:18–19 HCSB

Just because the world will be new, according to Anthony Hoekema, that doesn't mean you won't recognize anything or that your life here is pointless:

"This new earth will not be totally other than the present earth; it will be the present earth renewed and glorified, purged of all the results of sin. . . . In other words, there will be continuity as well as discontinuity between the present earth and the new earth. This implies that our life and work on this earth will have abiding significance for the new earth that is to come."

The prophet Isaiah makes predictions and promises about the future, but Hermann Gunkel shows how he requires a response from his readers right now, too:

"The prophet's powerful spirit pushes toward the final time and loves to paint the final condition graphically. They eagerly present the powerful jubilation into which Israel will break forth when the great [battle of the LORD] will take place and Zion will be redeemed. Or, they demand this rejoicing immediately."

Zooming **In**

A number of Eastern religions don't believe in the idea of either a re-created world or heaven. They believe in nirvana, more of a condition than a place, a condition where a person stops being an individual and becomes one with the universe. This is their goal, but without separation there is no worship or love or communication or appreciation.

The Old Testament Hebrew word for "new" used in Isaiah 65:17 is *chadash*. It has the meaning of "fresh" or "renewed." The New Testament Greek has two words, *kainos* and *neos*. Kainos means "totally new, never seen before." *Neos* means "made new" or "restored," like a historic house or a classic car.

Sometimes new things can be scary. Will they be good or bad? Even God can be scary. But he is always good.

Through the
Eyes of
Your Heart

Is there anything you hope God leaves the way it is in the new world he is going to create? Why?

_____

_____

_____

_____

What would you like to see changed in the new world God has promised? Why?

_____

_____

_____

_____

Are fear of the unknown and fear of change preventing you from enjoying what God may have in store for you even now?

_____

_____

_____

_____

How to Get What You Want

May He send you help from the sanctuary and sustain you from Zion. . . . May He give you what your heart desires and fulfill your whole purpose. Let us shout for joy at your victory and lift the banner in the name of our God. May the Lord fulfill all your requests.

Psalm 20:2, 4–5 HCSB

The Big Picture

Psalm 20 is both a song and a prayer. It is one of King David's war songs. That may seem strange, a song of war right there in the middle of a book of spiritual poems. But being a warrior's song doesn't make Psalm 20 any less spiritual. David knew that all of life was lived under the eye of God. He didn't view his spiritual life as something separate from the rest of life. So then, in the midst of conflict—whatever the conflict—David looked to God for his help. It is God who "sustains[s] you." It is God who "send[s] you help from the sanctuary." It is God who "give[s] you what your heart desire[s] and fulfill[s] your whole purpose." Imagine the confidence such a song would give a warrior going out to battle. Victory over enemies, the desires of your heart: here is the abundant life that God promises. Here is a God—and a life—worth fighting for.

As a song, this psalm would encourage the king and his army that God would be with them and bless and protect them and give them victory. But the psalm is also a prayer. As a prayer, it was asking God to do those things

take a **CLOSER** look for teens

David just said he would do, to go with the army, to bless and protect them and give them victory. Although this psalm talks a lot about the king, it has the soldiers and the people in mind, too. The first half of the psalm asks for and promises God's help, but the last half promises the people's response: "*we* will shout for joy," "*we* will lift up the banner," "*we* trust in the Lord," "*we* will rise up."

Like many psalms, this one does not have a date attached to it, so we do not know when it was written. David might have written it while he was king himself, to remind himself as he went into battle that he needed God's protection and blessing, and that God had promised him those things. Or he might have written it late in life, after he had named Solomon to replace him as king. The king who might have led the soldiers might change, but the idea is the same, the need for God's presence and protection and blessing.

Prayer is the soul's sincere desire.
James Montgomery

You might read "may he give you what your heart desires" and take it to mean that God will give you what you really, really want. God does give you the desires of your heart, not always by granting them, but sometimes by *determining* them. He transforms the person you are—including the desires of your heart—into the person he created you to be. Why? So you can "fulfill your whole purpose."

One of the benefits of an active prayer life is the fact that it is one important means by which God changes your way of thinking. Your hopes and desires come more and more into line with God's desires for you. When that is the case, the prayer "Thy kingdom come, thy will be done" is not a completely selfless prayer; it doesn't have to be. As your heart lines up with God's heart, you delight in the idea of God's will being done. You want nothing more than to fulfill the purpose God has for your life. God gives you the desires of your heart. That works two ways: he gives you what your heart desires, and he gives you the desires themselves.

> *We do not succeed in changing things according to our desire, but gradually our desire changes.*
>
> Marcel Proust

Why do you want what you want? Do you want what your parents or teachers or coaches want for you? Do friends or TV commercials give you ideas? Do you ever read a book or watch a movie and see what someone else has or does and make that—or avoiding the same thing—your purpose in life?

Apply It
to Your Life

God wants to give you "your whole purpose"—but that doesn't mean he will give you whatever you ask for. He wants to decide your goals for you. Face it, not everything you might dream of or ask for will necessarily be good for you. God wouldn't be doing you any favors if he gave you those things. He knows you—he knows everything—and when you ask for what is good for you, what is part of his plan for you, he will certainly give it to you. So, to get what you want . . . you need to want what God wants you to want.

Maybe that sounds weird, letting someone else decide for you what you ought to want. But God not only wants you to want what he wants, he really wants to give it to you, too.

Do what the LORD wants, and he will give you your heart's desire.

Psalm 37:4 CEV

How Others See It

C. S. Lewis understood the importance of desire—and God's willingness to give us the desires of our hearts—in the Christian life:

"There lurks in most modern minds the notion that to desire our own good and earnestly to hope for the enjoyment of it is a bad thing. [However], if we consider the unblushing promises of reward and the staggering nature of the rewards promised in the Gospels, it would seem that Our Lord finds our desires not too strong, but too weak. We are half-hearted creatures, fooling about with drink and sex and ambition when infinite joy is offered us, like an ignorant child who wants to go on making mud pies in a slum because he cannot imagine what is meant by the offer of a holiday at the sea. We are far too easily pleased."

Zooming **In**

In Old Testament times it was expected of the king that he would lead his armies into battle. Today, leaders usually stay at a safe distance and their generals fight for them, but then the king was expected to be brave and strong and give moral support and a good example to his soldiers.

There is a group of psalms called Royal Psalms or Kingship Psalms. These serve two purposes. Regarding the earthly king, they may ask God to bless him and give him wisdom to lead the people well. But most Royal Psalms also point toward God as the true King and toward Christ as the perfect King of the earth.

You usually know what you want. Sometimes it's harder to know what you ought to want. Sometimes you have to start with the desire to want what's right.

Through the
Eyes of
Your Heart

Do you have desires that you think God may not want to grant for you? Why wouldn't he?

_____

_____

_____

_____

In what ways do your friends and your society influence your desires? Are these things necessarily wrong? On the other hand, are they necessarily godly?

_____

_____

_____

Can you change your own desires to bring them in line with what God wants for you, or must he do it for you?

_____

_____

_____

The Taste Test

The Big Picture

Psalm 34 is another of David's psalms. This one, though, includes a little introduction; before the psalm itself begins, it is described in the text as "a psalm of David when he feigned madness before Abimelech." David's madness before the Philistine king Abimelech is not one of the better known of David's adventures, but it provides an interesting backdrop for this psalm.

This song was written before David was king. He had earned many supporters in the kingdom, and even King Saul's son, Jonathan, had befriended him and promised to support him. In the usual sequence of events, of course, Jonathan would be king after his father Saul, but Jonathan knew that David would someday become king in his place. And yet he loved David. When he learned that his father wanted to kill David, Jonathan warned his friend and sent him away from the king and the capital city.

David ended up in the Philistine city of Gath, of all places. This was the hometown of the giant Goliath, from that earlier adventure that everyone knows about. When the people of Gath heard David was among them, they got worried. The advisers to King Abimelech warned him. They knew that the Israelites sang songs about the tens of thousands of Philistines that David had killed. The Philistines referred to David as the king of the land, something not even every Israelite knew at that time.

David began to wonder whether Gath was a safe place to hide out after all. So he came up with a very unusual plan: he began to act like he was crazy. He drooled on himself and wrote on the walls so that the locals thought he was crazy. The plan worked. Abimelech decided that this drooling idiot was no threat after all. Instead of locking him up, he sent David away, saying that he already had enough crazy people in his kingdom.

That's what David's life was like. He was always living full throttle, always trusting not so much in his own abilities as in the God who had always shown himself to be faithful. When he sat down to write Psalm 34, David had just survived the threats of two different kings who had reason to kill him. But God delivered him, just as he always did. No wonder he was able to say, "Taste and see that the LORD is good"!

Truth is the trial of itself and
needs no other touch.
Ben Jonson

David was always living out there on the edge. That's exactly where he was able to find that God was faithful, not in the middle of his comfort zone. You wonder, in fact, if David even had a comfort zone. Psalm after psalm grew out of challenge and hardship and uncertainty—the kind of uncertainty that made David realize he had nowhere else to turn. For the first few decades of his life, David almost never enjoyed safety in any worldly sense. Danger and excitement were the order of the day. Still, David found peace and hope.

To paraphrase Mr. Beaver in *The Lion, the Witch, and the Wardrobe,* God is good, but he's not safe. God always delivers. He is always faithful. David found out that truth firsthand. Refusing to let God's goodness be a theological concept, David acted on his belief in God. He made the journey to Gath. He took a huge chance in acting crazy to fool the king into letting him go. But as David acted on his faith, he saw a good God making things work out in his favor. As he committed himself to a life that depended on God, he tasted for himself that God was good.

> *So they committed themselves to the will of God and resolved to proceed.*
>
> William Bradford

Sometimes you might be tempted to watch life from the sidelines, let others take the risks before committing to something. For some things, that might be a good idea. Watch someone do a crazy stunt before trying it yourself, and you might think twice. But you can't live all of your life that way. And you can't treat God that way. If you want to know God, sometimes you've just got to jump in with both feet.

Apply It
to Your Life

God is good. And though he will be patient with you in your weakness and even your doubt, he does not sit still for too much testing. You really need to buy in to him to find out how great he really is. The psalm doesn't say, "wait and see," but "taste and see" that God is good. And it's not like someone says, "Taste this; it's terrible." You can believe that without taking a taste. Sure, you've got to believe in something to put it in your mouth, and if it's something new, you may be taking a chance. But if you commit to God in a way as real and physical as taking a taste, you will find that he is good.

Commit yourselves to the LORD and serve him only, and he will deliver you.

1 Samuel 7:3 NIV

David Needham points out how accepting God's invitation and tasting him is a life-changing experience:

"God, who is aware of the infinity of his person and the impossibility of our ever fully comprehending or describing or defining him, says 'Come taste me! Just taste me, my son, my daughter. You'll see that I am good. And once you taste me, you're not going to worry about definitions quite so much anymore.'"

Believers can taste God at any and all times. John T. Faris says sometimes the experience is strongest during hard times:

"How those praises of the Lord are echoed by the Christian whose personal experience enables him or her to bear testimony to the goodness of God! Frequently that testimony will be given by someone lying on a bed of suffering. But there is no doubt in his heart. He knows that God is good, and whatever his trials may be, his one triumphant thought is *God's in his heaven; all's right with the world.*"

Zooming **In**

The same Hebrew root word, *Ta'am*, is used in Psalm 34 to refer both to David pretending to have lost his senses and to our relating to God with our senses. It's a pun, but it also means that you don't just "taste" God with your sense of taste, but you use your sense, your reason to appreciate him.

This psalm is an acrostic poem. Each verse begins with a different letter of the Hebrew alphabet. There are other psalms, like Psalm 119, the longest of the psalms, that do this, too. We miss much of it in English translation, but the psalms can be very complex. A lot of thought went into them.

God is good. He's so good, you can taste it. But only if you're willing to act on what you believe. Take a few minutes to reflect on your willingness to taste the goodness of God.

Would you rather test God from a distance and watch and see what he does, or are you ready to taste, to commit?

_____

_____

_____

What are ways you might give yourself halfheartedly to God without really committing to him?

_____

_____

_____

Why might you be reluctant to take the taste test with God? Are you afraid you will find he is not good, or are you not ready to buy into everything it would mean?

_____

_____

_____

Before You Know It

O Daniel, I have now come out to give you insight and understanding. At the beginning of your pleas for mercy a word went out, and I have come to tell it to you, for you are greatly loved.

Daniel 9:22–23 ESV

The Big Picture

It had been nearly seventy years since the people of Judah had been exiled to Babylon. They were strangers in a strange land, separated from the Promised Land that had defined them as a people for so many generations. Most of the Jews who were alive at that time had never seen the great temple at Jerusalem, which had been the center of their parents' lives. Most of the Jews had never known anything but Babylon, where strange customs prevailed and strange people ruled over them.

Daniel was one of those exiles. But he had an immediate hope that most of the Jews around him didn't have. He knew his Scripture, and from the book of Jeremiah he knew that the Exile was to last seventy years. He and his fellow Jews would soon be going home.

In preparation for that great day, he prayed to God. He confessed his sin and the sins of his people, seeking cleansing so that they might be ready to go back to the land God had promised to their forebears. While he was praying he received a most unexpected visitor—the angel Gabriel. Not only was the messenger unexpected, but he also brought an unexpected message: yes, they would soon be going back to Jerusalem. But they had far greater reason than that to hope and to rejoice. The Messiah was coming, Gabriel assured Daniel.

Daniel thought he was offering a pretty straightforward prayer: a prayer of confession, a prayer for wisdom, a prayer of restoration. But God's answer blows his doors off. "You want restoration, Daniel? Being restored to your homeland is nothing compared to the restoration I have planned through my Son, the Messiah. You want to confess your sins and get right with God? Here's my plan for washing away all your sin and making things right permanently." It's as if Daniel paddled out into the stream in his prayer canoe and God turned loose the dam and sent him shooting down the rapids—a joyous ride to be sure, but not the ride Daniel was bargaining for.

And then you notice that one little detail: "At the *beginning* of your pleas for mercy a word went out. . . ." God was sitting on ready, waiting to unleash this great news on Daniel as soon as he started praying.

*Prayer is a sincere, sensible, affectionate
pouring out of the soul to God, through Christ
in the strength and assistance of the Spirit,
for such things as God has promised.*

John Bunyan

Take a
Closer Look

Gabriel had appeared to Daniel before to explain a vision Daniel had about future events. He didn't expect or ask for him, but a voice in the vision sent Gabriel to Daniel. This time, Daniel had been reading the prophet Jeremiah and realized that the Exile was about to end, so he prayed to God, asking forgiveness for his own sins and the sins of his people. And Gabriel came to give Daniel more insight into future events. He told him he had been sent as soon as Daniel began his prayer. Not once God heard his request and decided it was reasonable, but as soon as he began his prayer. God knew Daniel would pray, and he knew his own response. Daniel's prayer did not persuade God as much as it was an event God required to happen before he made his next move. The same God who knows and plans and controls the world events Daniel saw in his visions knows and anticipates the prayers of your hearts. And he has his answers prepared. Just as he is ultimately good to his people in world events, his answers to your prayers will be good, too.

> *Prayer is not conquering God's reluctance, but taking hold of God's willingness.*
>
> Phillips Brooks

Prayer can be confusing. If you believe that God knows and controls everything, you might wonder if and how your prayers make any difference at all. But if your prayers can change God's plans, does he really know and control everything? The example of Daniel, though, shows that God is really the one in control. That doesn't mean your prayers don't matter. Gabriel would not have been sent to Daniel if he had not reached out to God in a prayer of confession.

God loves you and knows you and will answer your prayers. Maybe not in the way you want, but in the way he knows is best. That is a comforting idea. You might know times you prayed for something and thought God didn't answer, but eventually you saw that he had something better in store for you than what you were praying for. After all, Daniel prayed that the children of Israel might be allowed to go back to Jerusalem and rebuild the temple. But Gabriel told Daniel about the coming of Christ. It was mysterious, and you might not always understand, but God knows what he's doing, and what he is doing includes your prayers.

He answered their prayers, because they trusted in him.
1 Chronicles 5:20 NIV

How Others
See It

Tricia McCary Rhodes wrote an excellent book on prayer called *Intimate Intercession*. She begins her book with a "What if . . ." thought experiment:

"What if we really believed that intercession is more about fulfilling our destiny than completing some kind of Christian obligation? What if we believed that praying for others is akin to embarking on the greatest adventure of all, rather than living up to some nebulous spiritual standard? What if, instead of racking up successes or cataloging our failures, we lived in a state of awe that the Lord of the universe has invited us to join him in the dance of life? Maybe we would decide at last to pick up the gauntlet God continually throws down before us and accept his dare—to just ask for his glory and our joy."

Zooming **In**

Gabriel is one of only two angels in the Bible we know of by name. The other is Michael. Gabriel is God's chief messenger angel. He appeared twice to Daniel. He announced the birth of John the Baptist. And he is the one who told Mary that she would be the mother of the Messiah.

Nebuchadnezzar of Babylon first attacked Jerusalem in 605 BC. That is when Daniel and his friends were taken back to Babylon. Eight years later, the Jews rebelled and Nebuchadnezzar replaced King Jehoiachin with Zedekiah, his uncle. In 586 BC, after another rebellion, Nebuchadnezzar destroyed the city and the temple. Cyrus of Persia gave the decree to return in 538 BC.

Prayer is one of the most important things you can do as a Christian. But it can also confuse and frustrate you. God surely hears and replies in his own all-powerful way.

If God knows your prayers and has his answers prepared before you pray them, why do you think he requires that you pray?

Do you believe God knows your prayers before you pray them, or do you try to be as persuasive as possible?

How does it make you feel to think that God has planned a response to your prayer before you pray it?

Who Is There in the Dark?

The LORD is my shepherd; I shall not want. He makes me lie down in green pastures. He leads me beside still waters. He restores my soul. He leads me in paths of righteousness for his name's sake. Even though I walk through the valley of the shadow of death, I will fear no evil, for you are with me; your rod and your staff, they comfort me.

Psalm 23:1–4 ESV

The **Big Picture**

David was a man who knew hard times. As the youngest son, he wasn't always remembered or appreciated. As a shepherd, he was often alone in open fields. He had to fight lions and bears. As a young boy, not yet old enough to be a soldier, he fought and killed a giant who had the Israelite army paralyzed with fear. He was invited to live with the king . . . but then the king tried again and again to kill him! First, he challenged him to fight battles that would have gotten a lesser man killed. When that didn't work, he started throwing spears at him. So David left the king and ran for his life. Again he was sleeping in open fields. Again he had to face wild animals. And now he was considered a runaway criminal. To be safe from his own king, he had to hide in the countries of the people he used to fight. His life was not safe.

It's not as if his problems went away once he became king, either. The soldiers of the former king did not come to his side without a fight. At one point, when power went to David's head, he started acting like any other corrupt king of his era instead of a servant of God. He took another man's wife and had the man killed to cover up the crime. When that woman had a baby, it died. Among the many other children David had by several wives, one son, Amnon, abused his half sister, Tamar, and Absalom, another son of David, killed him for it. Later, Absalom even rebelled against David himself and the king had to leave Jerusalem, his capital city, in the middle of the night. Again he was running for his life.

It has been suggested that it was during this time that David wrote Psalm 23. He'd had to run for his life before, but not from his own son. When he ran from Saul, David had the promise of God that he would be king in his place. He was not sure what would be the result of Absalom's revolt. This might be the end of his reign as king. But whatever happened, he knew that God was good, even during the hardest times, during life's biggest challenges.

No coward soul is mine, no trembler in the world's storm-troubled sphere: I see Heaven's glories shine, and faith shines equal, arming me from fear.

Emily Brontë

When this familiar song of comfort begins, it is speaking of God, not directly as "you" but as "the LORD," the way you speak about someone who's not in the room at the time. It says good things about him: he provides, gives, directs. He gives material provision, like food and water, and he gives rest when you are weary. He also gives spiritual direction, leading you in paths of righteousness.

But in verse 4, the psalm changes from "he" to "you." As David thinks about the valley of the shadow of death, he is not afraid, because God is with him. And realizing that he is with him, David can no longer speak of God as if he's not there. He is! "I will fear no evil." Why not? "For *you* are with me." David does not say, "He is with me." At the times you need God the most, he is most obviously there, and you cannot help but turn to him and thank him. This psalm is popular for God's people in times of trial, like times of war or at the death of a loved one, because God is sometimes closest in life's hardest times.

> *Behind the dim unknown, standeth God within the shadow, keeping watch above his own.*
>
> James Russell Lowell

You may encounter hard times or difficult circumstances. David did. You may not fight lions or bears or giants, but you may have a friend or family member who dies, goes to war, gets divorced. You may get sick yourself, or be betrayed or rejected, even by old friends.

Apply It
to Your Life

Never forget that God is always there during the dark times. Sometimes you may think you can get along pretty well without him. And when things are going well for you, you might be able to. But when things get tough, when you feel alone, you can look around and see the God who is there. You might turn to him and say, "You are with me." When you get close enough to God that you learn to talk directly to him, life's next challenge won't be so frightening.

I am persuaded that neither death nor life, nor angels nor rulers, nor things present, nor things to come, nor powers, nor height, nor depth, nor any other created thing will have the power to separate us from the love of God that is in Christ Jesus our Lord!

Romans 8:38–39 HCSB

The fact that God is with you in the Valley of the Shadow does not mean that it is not scary, as John Calvin points out:

"Surely it is terrifying to walk in the darkness of death and believers, whatever their strength may be, cannot but be frightened by it. But since the thought prevails that they have God beside them, caring for their safety, fear at once yields to assurance. However great are the devices, as Augustine says, that the devil throws up against us . . . where faith dwells, he is cast out."

Henry Gariepy shows how, in addition to his presence, God often provides things and circumstances to comfort and encourage you in hard times:

"Valleys need not be forbidding places. They are most often well watered, with rich feed and forage along the route. As we come to this valley, we will find even there provision to sustain us, enabling us to pass through.

"Death is not substance, but shadow. It is not the valley of death, but the valley of the *shadow* of death. Where there is shadow, there must be light."

Zooming In

The Hebrew phrase *salmawet*, translated "shadow of death," doesn't necessarily need to mean death or dying, but might just be a way to say very, very dark shadows or darkness. Shepherds in Israel sometimes needed to lead their flocks in ravines so deep the sun was hidden, and it was very dark.

The image of the king as a shepherd was somewhat common in the ancient Near East in Bible times. The powerful Hammurabi, king of Babylon around 1700 BC, called himself a shepherd. One of Babylon's gods, Shamash, the god of justice, was also considered guardian of the upper world, or heaven, and shepherd of the lower world, earth.

Life dishes out hard times for everybody. But David experienced the closeness of God in a real way more often during the hard times than during better times.

What is a dark, shadowy time you have been through? Did you feel God was closer to you then than at other times?

_____

_____

_____

_____

In your life, do you spend more time talking *about* God, as "him," or talking *to* God, as "you"?

_____

_____

_____

_____

How does the thought that you might be more aware of God's nearness make hard times easier to face?

_____

_____

_____

_____

Too Good to Be True?

> *He showed them His hands and His feet. While they still could not believe it because of their joy and amazement, He said to them, "Have you anything here to eat?" They gave Him a piece of a broiled fish; and He took it and ate it before them.*

Luke 24:40–43 NASB

The Big Picture

Jesus' followers were discouraged and doubtful in the days after his death, and it's not hard to imagine why. They had hoped he would be a liberator king who would overthrow the Romans and put the Jews in charge. Some of them had understood that he was the Son of God, some had not, but all who followed him had willingly cut themselves off from the established religious and cultural order. They had pinned all of their hopes on him. And now Jesus was dead. The disciples didn't know where to turn.

Three days after Jesus died, his followers began hearing reports that he had come back to life. They remembered that he had promised several times to return from the dead. But then again, Jesus had said a lot of things his followers didn't understand. Had he been using a figure of speech? Was he talking about Judgment Day at the end of time? What if he himself had made a mistake? The disciples wanted to believe, but they were hearing some pretty wild stories from some obviously excited people.

That evening, the disciples gathered to talk about what they had heard and seen. And suddenly, while they were talking, Jesus appeared to them. The door didn't open; in fact, it was still locked. Jesus was just simply there. They could tell it was Jesus easily enough. Some of them had lived with him for years. The fresh wounds in his hands and feet told them that this was the Jesus whom they had seen die a few days earlier. But they still couldn't believe he was alive and well and talking to them. People don't just come back from the dead. They were afraid he was a ghost. But Jesus reassured them. He ate a piece of broiled fish, something a ghost couldn't do. And the disciples were finally convinced that this was their teacher and friend, and that he was right in front of them—in the flesh. The disciples had always been a little slow to understand the things that Jesus had shown and told them. Now disappointment and sorrow, it appeared, had further hardened their hearts so that they couldn't trust their eyes. In the end, however, they had no choice but to believe.

Your wildest dreams aren't wild enough—not nearly as extravagant as the joys God offers his people.

Jonathan Rogers

Dead people don't raise themselves back to life, do they? The disciples saw Jesus raise Lazarus and others from the dead, but that was different: he was alive when he did that. It's not like the disciples thought Jesus was some kind of zombie. They were just freaked out because he died at all. Someone so powerful should have been able to avoid death altogether. Once he was dead, even he couldn't help himself. Could he? They were afraid they had put all of their hope in a loser.

Then he appeared. Luke says their "joy and amazement" kept them from believing it was really him. It wasn't just fear or doubt that they felt. They also felt joy. And even the joy made it hard to believe. Could something so good really be true? Maybe all wasn't lost after all. They really wanted to believe, even when it didn't make sense. But Luke says their joy kept them from believing. In other words, they didn't want to get their hopes up. Jesus coming back to life would solve a lot of problems, but that's what made it hard. Maybe this was all just wishful thinking. In the end, the disciples did come to believe and ditched their doubt. But they never lost their joy or their amazement.

God never made a promise that was too good to be true.

Dwight L. Moody

You know the drill. You spend half your time daydreaming about all the great things you wish would happen to you—a starting position, true love, self-confidence, your parents' approval. You spend the other half of your time pretending you don't care. Life has its disappointments. So you learn to shrug things off. You mumble, "Whatever," and you keep on going. You learn not to hope for too much. Only a sucker goes for a deal that seems too good to be true.

Apply It
to Your Life

But if you let that kind of thinking carry over to your relationship with Jesus, you're going to miss out on the life he came to give you. Does the good news of Jesus sound too good to be true? In earthly terms, it probably is. And yet, what if it *is* true? What if Jesus really did come back from the dead to bring new life to people who are messed up, people who are crippled by the fear of being rejected? It's time to switch out of self-protection mode. You can accept the gospel or you can reject the gospel. But you can't just shrug and say, "Whatever."

I believe the promise God made to our people long ago. . . . Why should any of you doubt that God raises the dead to life?

Acts 26:6, 8 CEV

How Others See It

Some people find the gospel hard to believe because "there's no such thing as a free lunch." Everything else in life has to be paid for or worked for. But, as Charles Swindoll points out, that's not what grace means. (This quote from Swindoll begins with a quote from pastor Donald Barnhouse.)

"'Love that goes upward is worship; love that goes outward is affection; love that stoops is grace.' To show grace is to extend favor or kindness to one who doesn't deserve it and can never earn it. Receiving God's acceptance by grace always stands in sharp contrast to earning it on the basis of works. Every time the thought of grace appears, there is the idea of its being undeserved. In no way is the recipient getting what he or she deserves. Favor is being extended simply out of the goodness of the heart of the giver."

Zooming In

There are temples all over the world where offerings can be made to different gods. It is the job of some priests to clean off the old fruit, grain, flowers, incense, and all the other kinds of offerings because the gods never come to eat them. Jesus ate fish with his disciples. He was not a ghost, but God with man.

Some like the idea of reincarnation—the idea that death is the door to another life much like this one. Maybe they were rich or famous in the past, or might be the next time around. But religions that teach this idea say life is hard. Who wants to go through it again? Jesus' resurrected body was perfect, without pain or hurt, and yours will be, too.

Jesus' resurrection was awesome news for his disciples. Two thousand years later, it's still awesome. It almost seems too good to be true. But it's not. God is really that good and true.

Through the
Eyes of
Your Heart

When something good happens to you, do you wait for the other shoe to drop? Do you feel that anything good that happens to you is going to be balanced out by something bad? Where does that kind of thinking come from?

_____

_____

_____

Do you think you have to have it all together before God will start to do things in your life? Is that true? Was it for the disciples?

_____

_____

_____

_____

If Jesus did come back to life, what does that have to do with you? What does it mean for you in everyday life?

_____

_____

_____

_____

Is God Bigger Than Human Disagreements?

> Some time later Paul said to Barnabas, "Let us go back and visit the brothers in all the towns where we preached the word of the Lord and see how they are doing." Barnabas wanted to take John, also called Mark, with them, but Paul did not think it wise to take him.

Acts 15:36–38 NIV

The Big Picture

The first time Paul appears in the New Testament, he is persecuting the church. The first time Barnabas appears, he is encouraging new believers and teaching them. The name Barnabas, in fact, is a nickname meaning "Son of Encouragement." Not a likely pair, right? But God turned Paul's life around, and Barnabas, true to form, welcomed him into the church. They did a couple of jobs together for the church. Then the Holy Spirit spoke to church leaders at a prayer meeting and announced that Paul and Barnabas should go on a trip to spread the gospel. They took along Barnabas's young cousin Mark as a helper. Their early mission was a great success. On the island of Cyprus, in miraculous circumstances, they saw the governor become a Christian! After they sailed on from there, Mark decided to go back home, but Paul and Barnabas continued on and had more success, starting a number of churches.

Several years later, Paul suggested to Barnabas that they take a second journey. He wanted to visit the churches they had started and see how they were doing. Barnabas agreed, and wanted to take Mark with them again. The Bible does not say why Mark left them on their first trip, but it apparently upset Paul very much, and he did not want to take him on their second trip. Was Paul's earlier hard side coming out again? Was it the differences in their personalities finally showing through? In any case, Paul and Barnabas had such an argument that they separated, and they ended up taking two separate trips. Barnabas took Mark and sailed for Cyprus, the same way their earlier trip had begun. Paul took a man named Silas and went north and traveled by land this time to the same places he had been before. On their way, they passed through Paul's hometown of Tarsus. Though it got off to a rocky start, this missionary journey was also a success. Paul and Silas founded a number of churches that would be historically important and inspire at least three books of the Bible. They also met Timothy, who would become a pastor and leader in the early church and would have a couple of books of the Bible named for him, too. Acts doesn't talk more about Barnabas and Mark's trip, but we know that they continued in faithful service to God and caught up with Paul later on. The argument between Paul and Barnabas seems to show that even people working for God can argue with one another, but God gets his work done anyway.

And sheathed their swords
for lack of argument.

William Shakespeare

Paul and Barnabas weren't perfect. Probably both of them were to blame for their argument. But here's what's cool about the split between Paul and Barnabas: through it, God made a way for two missionary journeys instead of only one. God used differences of opinion, even an argument, to double the number of missionaries.

Even after the split, things did not go the way Paul expected. First he wanted to preach in Asia, but he couldn't. God stopped him from going to Bithynia, too. Paul ended up going to Macedonia, a place he never planned to go; it proved to be an important moment in the history of the early church.

The Bible doesn't say what Barnabas and Mark did in the end, but if they followed their original plan and continued in the direction they were traveling, they would have gone back to the churches they started on the first trip and encouraged them.

Eventually, Paul and Barnabas and Mark all made up again. Mark even became Paul's sidekick and helped support him when he was in prison in Rome. God used a fight to get twice as much work done, and brought everyone back together again to prove that they were all on the same side after all.

> Whenever you're in conflict with someone, there is one factor that can make the difference between damaging your relationship and deepening it. That factor is attitude.
>
> William James

You know what it's like to have disagreements with parents, brothers and sisters, teachers and friends. People fight about all kinds of things: are you getting respect, are you being treated fairly, are you being told what to do? Sometimes people even fight about how they should serve God. But God's plan for you might not be for someone else, and you shouldn't try to get them to follow with you, or fight if they won't.

Here's one thing you can learn from Paul's fight with Barnabas: God has a plan, and he can use you to get it done even if you don't have a clue. So when you run into speed bumps or have hassles with friends, try stepping back from the situation and taking a big-picture look at things. What might God be trying to use you to do? It might not be the same thing he is going to do through your friend. If you have different jobs to do, think of how you can help your friend do his or her job instead of arguing. You might need to make some changes in your plans, too, to do your job without your friend's help.

You're blessed when you can show people how to cooperate instead of compete or fight. That's when you discover who you really are, and your place in God's family.

Matthew 5:9 MSG

Martin Luther actually finds hope in the story of the church's first missionaries fighting:

How Others
See It

"Here it appears either Paul or Barnabas went too far. It must have been a violent disagreement to separate two associates who were so closely united. Indeed, the text indicates as much.

"Such examples are written for our consolation: for it is a great comfort to us to hear that great saints, who have the Spirit of God, also struggle. Those who say that saints do not sin would deprive us of this comfort."

John Gill sees in this passage in Acts how God still manages to bring good out of something we see as bad:

"It is not easy to say which was to blame most in this contention; perhaps there were faults on both sides, for the best men are not without their failings; yet this affair was overruled by the providence of God, for the spread of his Gospel, and the enlargement of his interest; for when these two great and good men parted from one another, they went to different places, preaching the word of God."

Zooming In

With the conversion of the proconsul in AD 45, Cyprus had the world's first Christian governor. There is a monastery on the island, built in the fifth century to commemorate the discovery of Barnabas's bones. Wars and invasions have changed the political situation on Cyprus repeatedly, but the church has always been there and continues today.

Many people believe that the Mark in this story from Acts wrote the second Gospel. He probably wrote down what Peter dictated, probably during the time Peter was in Rome, under arrest. The Gospel has many Latin features and figures of speech that would accommodate a Roman audience and show Mark's missionary character, even in writing.

Messed-up people in a messed-up world will sometimes disagree, sometimes even fight. But God brings them together in the end. And isn't it great to know that God has an awesome plan that even your hot temper can't stop? He even uses mistakes and weaknesses as part of that plan.

There's a good chance you're in conflict with somebody right now. What kind of good could you imagine God bringing out of that conflict? What good has he brought out of conflicts in the past?

_____

_____

_____

It's human nature: your first reaction when someone has a different opinion is to think, "I'm right, this person is wrong." How is it possible that people with two different opinions could both be serving God?

_____

_____

_____

Sometimes, however, you really do find yourself in a conflict where one person is right and one person is wrong. How do you know the difference between that kind of conflict and a simple difference of opinion? How do you handle it differently?

_____

_____

What Jesus Really Wanted

When the hour had come, He reclined at the table, and the apostles with Him. And He said to them, "I have earnestly desired to eat this Passover with you before I suffer; for I say to you, I shall never again eat it until it is fulfilled in the kingdom of God."

Luke 22:14–16 NASB

The Big Picture

Passover memorializes the night in Egypt when God's angel brought death to all the firstborn Egyptian males but left the firstborn Hebrew boys untouched. The Hebrews smeared the blood of lambs on their doorposts as a sign of their faith, and the angel of death "passed over" them. They were delivered, quite literally, by the blood of the lamb.

Every year, on the anniversary of this event, the Jews celebrated the Passover again. They ate lamb to remember the blood that saved them. They ate bitter herbs to remember the bitterness of slavery in Egypt. And they ate flat bread made without yeast, to remember the hurry of that first Passover night, when they didn't even have time to let their bread rise before leaving on their journey to the Promised Land. The meal reminded them of how God had freed them in the past and how he would free them again in the future.

It is not hard to see why Passover is so important to the Jews. Nor should it be surprising that so many important events in Jesus' life and ministry occurred at Passover. The only Bible story about Jesus' childhood—the time his parents accidentally left him at the temple in Jerusalem—happened at Passover. Jesus whipped the money changers out of the temple on a Passover. He fed five thousand people with five loaves of bread and two fish one Passover, then he walked across the Sea of Galilee.

Jesus' last Passover on earth, however, was his most important. He celebrated the Passover meal with his disciples the night before he was crucified. He spoke ominously to the disciples: "I shall never again eat it [the Passover] until it is fulfilled in the kingdom of God." The disciples had no way of knowing that the fulfillment Jesus spoke of would happen in less than twenty-four hours. All those slaughtered lambs of the Passover and the whole sacrificial system were only a foreshadowing of the sacrifice that would happen on the hill at Golgotha. But this one would be a perfect sacrifice. This one would actually fulfill God's requirements. This sacrifice would free God's people from slavery and from death once and for all. On that last Passover, he became the perfect sacrifice; the Passover lambs of all those years were only a pale shadow, a little preview of Jesus, the Lamb of God, whose blood not only delivers his people from death, but also frees them from slavery.

To see the law by Christ fulfilled, to hear his pardoning voice, changes a slave into a child, and duty into choice.

William Cowper

Take a closer look at that clause, "I have earnestly desired to eat this Passover with you." It's the sort of thing you might say at any holiday—"I've been looking forward to this for months," or "It's just so great to be here with the family again." But it quickly became obvious that Jesus was talking about something else, something deeper when he said, "I have earnestly desired . . ." He has earnestly desired this Passover because it represents the completion of his work on earth. This Passover was the grand finale in more ways than one. Jesus knew it would be his last before he returned to heaven. But more important, this Passover would be the culmination of the fourteen hundred or so Passovers that had gone before.

Jesus did not only end the Passover, though. He replaced it with something. He had taught earlier that anyone who wanted the salvation he was offering would need to eat his flesh and drink his blood. It sounded creepy at the time, but when Jesus introduced the same idea at the Lord's Supper it was to show a new way that God would bring salvation to his people.

Jesus did not look forward to his death. He was in agony that he would become sin and be separated from God. He would pray in a few hours that God not require him to die, even though he knew he must. But his desire to see his people saved was so great that he couldn't wait to make it happen.

> Have your heart right with Christ, and he will visit you often, and so turn weekdays into Sundays, meals into sacraments, homes into temples and earth into heaven.
>
> C. H. Spurgeon

This is not a *What Would Jesus Do* situation. Only Jesus could replace the Passover because only he was the Lamb of God. But he gives you a great example in his intense commitment to follow God's will. In the short term, what Jesus had to do would be horrible. He would be arrested, beaten, mocked, condemned, and killed. But he wanted to

do it because this sacrifice of himself was the very reason he had come to earth as a man. He needed this last meal with his followers, not only to try to explain the events that were coming and share with them a few parting truths, but to share this meal that symbolized his love for them, for all mankind.

God has something planned for you. It may be something hard, something you wouldn't ordinarily want to do. Can you commit yourself to doing what God wants? Think about this act of obedience as Christ did. He didn't concentrate on the pain it would mean for him. He thought about how the disciples and the millions to follow would benefit. And he thought about how his obedience would please his heavenly Father. And he knew that in the end he would be with God once again. And so he obeyed.

It cost God plenty to get you out of that dead-end, empty-headed life you grew up in. He paid with Christ's sacred blood, you know. He died like an unblemished, sacrificial lamb.

1 Peter 1:18–19 MSG

In his intense desire to share the Last Supper with the disciples, Jesus displayed his human side. He wanted their company and comfort, according to Matthew Henry:

"See the love he had to his disciples; he desired to eat it with them, that he and they might have a little time together for private conversation. He was not about to leave them, but was very desirous to *eat this Passover with them before he suffered,* as if the comfort of that would carry him the more cheerfully through his sufferings."

David Guzik points out how Jesus is ready to get on with the Lord's Supper because it changes everything:

"The fervent desire Jesus mentions is for good reason; it isn't so much that He is saying 'goodbye' to His disciples, as much as He is coming to the entire reason why He came—to institute a new covenant with man, on the basis of His own sacrifice. This is not the beginning of the end, it is the beginning of the beginning."

Zooming In

The Passover service a Jewish family celebrates in their home is called the Seder. Seder means "order"; the service must be done in a certain order. The service tells the story of the Exodus from Egypt. Children participate in telling the story by asking and answering specific questions. Symbolic foods also make the story more dramatic and memorable.

In the early church, the Lord's Supper may have been a full meal. There was a tradition known as the Love Feast, in which the believers sat down to a meal together. It's not entirely clear whether this Love Feast was the Lord's Supper itself or an additional celebration. Paul had to scold the Corinthians for letting the Love Feast turn into an occasion for excessive eating and drinking.

Jesus did something only he could do when he replaced the Passover with the Lord's Supper. He is a great example of obedience and faithfulness.

Do you desire to do what God wants you to do, even if it seems unpleasant?

_____

_____

_____

_____

How can Christ's example help you do things that might not be painful, but only boring or annoying?

_____

_____

_____

_____

Jesus knew that he would suffer pain soon, but concentrated on the reward that would come after. How can his example help you desire to obey God, even in hard times?

_____

_____

_____

Worth Doing Well

People were overwhelmed with amazement. "He has done everything well," they said. "He even makes the deaf hear and the mute speak."

Mark 7:37 NIV

The Big Picture

When Jesus was in the city of Decapolis, some people brought a man to him who needed healing. He was deaf and spoke with difficulty. They begged Jesus to "lay His hand on him" (Mark 7:32 NASB). The friends of the deaf-mute man had heard of Jesus' healings; perhaps some of them had witnessed healing. They were confident that Jesus could help if only he would lay a hand on the man.

Jesus did more than lay a hand on the man. He stuck his fingers in the man's ears. Then Jesus spat on his finger and touched the saliva to the man's tongue. It sounds a little gross, but it worked. Jesus called out, "Be opened!" and the man could hear and talk as plainly as anyone else.

Miracles such as that would appear to be publicity bonanzas for a Man who was trying to spread a new and better message. What better way to get word-of-mouth started? *Thank you, thank you. If you enjoyed the show, don't forget to tell your friends. I'll be here in Decapolis all week. Media inquiries should be directed to . . .* But that's not what Jesus did. Jesus "gave them orders not to tell anyone" (7:36 NASB). For some reason, he still wanted his true identity and his true purpose to be a secret. He instituted a gag order.

But how are people supposed to keep quiet when they see one man heal another man's lifelong affliction with two fingers and a little bit of spit? Maybe the people tried to keep quiet, but it wasn't long before they were proclaiming the news widely. They couldn't help it. You wonder especially about the man who could speak for the first time. Did he not use his newly freed tongue to tell the amazing story of the Man who healed him? Even if he did obey Jesus' orders not to tell what happened, the very fact that a deaf man could now talk was a testimony to Jesus' power.

"He has done everything well," the people marveled. They were just talking about his incredible ability to heal the deaf and the mute. They probably didn't know how true their statement was. Jesus did more than just heal well. He did *everything* well.

Servant of God, well done, well hast thou
fought the better fight.

John Milton

Jesus did many miracles and everyone was amazed. But Jesus did more than work miracles. He lived life and lived it well. He was praised as a baby for being pretty exceptional. As a child neither God nor man could find anything wrong with him or what he did. And in his ministry religious leaders always focused on certain technical points in their law (not God's law), but could find nothing wrong with him as a person. And his supporters said he had done *all things* well. He didn't just preach and teach and heal. He walked and talked and ate meals and slept and prayed and visited people. And absolutely *everything* he did, he did well. He didn't consider anything unimportant or not worth doing well. He didn't neglect certain things so he could concentrate on what might have been considered more "important." He considered all things important because his mission was to preach and teach and heal, but also to live an obedient life. His character, his behavior, and his good deeds were part of his obedience as much as keeping the law of Moses.

> *He preaches well that lives well.*
>
> Miguel de Cervantes

You know the saying, "Practice what you preach." It's even been said that it's important to practice *before* you preach. People notice the things you do and how you do them. If you do what is good and right, and if you do it well, it will affect whether or not people listen to what you say. It's easy sometimes to say that certain things aren't important enough to do, or if you have to do them you might want to do them halfheartedly or in a sloppy or careless way. But Jesus didn't see anything that way.

Apply It
to Your Life

Jesus did *all things* well, because he knew that people were watching and anything he did poorly would undermine his message. But he also knew that everything that came his way came from God and presented an opportunity to serve and please God. The same is true for you. You probably don't think of chores as worship or homework as a chance to bring glory to God, but it's true. God is God over everything. And when you see him as Jesus did, doing everything well isn't too much to ask.

Well done, good and faithful servant. You have been faithful over a little; I will set you over much. Enter into the joy of your master.

Matthew 25:21 ESV

Walter W. Wessel sees in Jesus' miracles and the people's response a parallel to God's work in creating the world:

"Another result of the healing was that the people were 'overwhelmed.' The statement 'he has done everything well' reminds us of Genesis 1:31: 'God saw all that he made, and it was very good.' The reminder is not unsuitable, for in a profound sense, Jesus' work is indeed 'a new creation.'"

Saint Ambrose summarized the excellence of Christ in the following way:

"When we speak about wisdom, we are speaking about Christ. When we speak about virtue, we are speaking about Christ. When we speak about justice, we are speaking about Christ. When we speak about peace, we are speaking about Christ. When we speak about truth and life and redemption, we are speaking about Christ."

Zooming In

Fanny Crosby wrote more than 8,000 hymns. One of them is "All the Way, My Savior Leads Me," which includes the line: "I know, whatever befalls me, Jesus doeth all things well." She was blind from the time she was six weeks old but was a woman famous for her exceptional faith and spiritual insight.

Jesus always had popular support for what he *did*. Even when he cleaned out the temple with a whip, he upset the ruling religious leaders, but not the crowds. They were always happy to be fed and healed by him. What upset the crowds, eventually, was what Jesus *said*: that he was the Son of God, that they needed to eat his flesh and drink his blood, that he would die and be raised.

> *What you do can be as important*
> *as what you say and so can the*
> *way you do it.*

Do you make an effort to do all things well, not just those that seem to have religious significance?

_____

_____

_____

_____

Do you believe anything worth doing is worth doing well? What are some things you may be tempted to do halfway?

_____

_____

_____

_____

How does the way you do everything—spiritual or religious or just plain and ordinary—have an impact on the things you say and whether people believe you or not?

_____

_____

_____

Mustard Seeds and Miracles

The apostles said to the Lord, "Make our faith stronger!" Jesus replied: If you had faith no bigger than a tiny mustard seed, you could tell this mulberry tree to pull itself up, roots and all, and to plant itself in the ocean. And it would!

Luke 17:5–6 CEV

The Big Picture

Jesus was on his way to Jerusalem for the last time. He knew he was going to be crucified, so his teaching got more intense. He had been teaching his disciples about the kingdom of God. He told them what it would cost them to be his disciples. He told them, too, about God's gracious forgiveness for sinners, and how much rejoicing there is in heaven when one sinner turns away from sin and turns to God. He spoke on the danger of living only for material wealth. And he gave them a parable to illustrate how God's judgment for sin will be permanent and irreversible.

The disciples had been with Jesus now for nearly two years. They may have felt that they had made good decisions so far. They knew they were not worthy of the kingdom, but were there by God's grace. They had experienced the cost of discipleship and thought they could handle it. They certainly didn't have material wealth that might drag them down spiritually. Because of all of these things, they hoped to avoid God's judgment and its eternal consequences.

When Jesus started talking about interpersonal relationships, however, things started to get a little heavy. *You're going to offend each other,* Jesus said. *And when you do, you're going to have to be ready to forgive one another.* Jesus went so far as to say, "If [your brother] sins against you seven times in a day, and seven times comes back to you and says, 'I repent,' forgive him" (Luke 17:4 NIV). That seems to be what really hit home for the disciples. That teaching about super-human forgiveness is what made them say, "Whoa, we can't possibly do this on our own." So they asked Jesus, "Increase our faith."

Jesus told them all it takes is the faith of a mustard seed, the smallest of seeds. That's a remarkable statement. The disciples said, "Increase our faith!" Jesus said, "You don't need a bigger faith. You need faith in a bigger God." If they had that kind of faith, he said, they would be able to pull up trees by the roots—just using the power of their will—and they would be able to order the trees planted in the sea.

The beginning of anxiety is the end of faith, and the beginning of true faith is the end of anxiety.

George Müller

With faith, you can command a tree to be planted in the sea. Not sunk in the sea, not drowned, but planted. Trees don't normally grow in the sea. But this is Jesus' way of describing the amazing results that are possible with faith in God. It is not just that things go your way. The result of faith is not that ordinary things happen for you sooner or better. With faith in God you will see supernatural results. You will see miracles.

After all, what makes these things happen is not the faith itself. What matters is not the amount of faith or how strong it is. Jesus talks about faith as small as a mustard seed, and that's pretty puny. What matters is the object of the faith, God himself. God works miracles. The disciples think Jesus has asked them to do something impossible and they need special help. But overcoming your selfish heart so that you humbly come to him in the first place was a miracle. And when you need the strength to forgive someone who has sinned against you or hurt you, God gives the miraculous ability to do that, too.

> *Miracles and truth are necessary, because it is necessary to convince the entire man, in body and soul.*
>
> Blaise Pascal

Do you have the faith of a mustard seed? That may be one of those sayings of Jesus that make you wonder what he really means. But do you have even a little faith? Jesus teaches that just a little faith can work miracles. Not just any faith, not just faith in *anything*, but faith in the God of the Bible. When you pray for something, do you expect God to act? Do you wonder how he is going to arrange perfectly natural and predictable events in your favor?

Apply It to Your Life

Jesus didn't tell his disciples about the tree in the ocean for the sake of moving trees. He wanted to make a powerful point. His point is that God can give you the strength to forgive someone, even when you think they've gone beyond what is reasonable. The God of the Bible is a God of miracles—even in human relationships. Do you think you can never forgive the person who abused you, or the parent who abandoned you, or the "friend" who told lies about you in school, or the guy or girl who broke your heart? He can. God can and will give you the strength to do the impossible. All you need is faith the size of a mustard seed. Faith in the God of the Bible. God will work to change your heart, and he is capable of changing the hearts of those who've hurt you.

The good news tells how God accepts everyone who has faith, but only those who have faith.

Romans 1:17 CEV

God does not give believers whatever they ask for just because of their faith. Dr. Ralph F. Wilson reminds us that Jesus' teaching on the power of faith is about forgiveness:

Jesus says "you are able to uproot the most tenacious tree and plant it, and make it grow where no tree can possibly grow. Jesus is not encouraging his disciples to do some capricious miracle. . . . They say they don't have enough faith to forgive as much or as long as he says they must. He replies that they have more than enough faith to do this.

In *The Weathering Grace of God*, Ken Gire compares the prayer of faith to the planting of a seed:

"Each time we pray, we plant a seed. It takes years to sow them. Even more to grow them. . . . We plant them in faith, not knowing how many will sprout, or of those that sprout, how many will survive. And though the odds are against us, we believe that some of those seeds will take root, that some of them will survive, and that someday they will make a difference in the landscape of our lives."

Zooming **In**

Black mustard, the kind of mustard that grows in Israel, can grow up to twelve feet tall. It is grown for its seeds, which are only 1/25 of an inch in size. The seeds have oils that can be eaten as a condiment, or used as a lubricant, or made into soap. Mustard oil is also used in cat and dog repellents.

When Jesus told his disciples to "forgive," he used the word *aphiemi*. It literally means "send away." The idea behind forgiveness, then, is to "send away" another person's wrong. Rather than hanging on to it, or letting it weigh you down, you get rid of it. It's a matter of freeing yourself of the wrong as much as it's a matter of freeing the person who has wronged you.

God works miracles, sometimes in response to your prayers. Even a little faith in a big God can do amazing things.

Through the
Eyes of
Your Heart

Do you ever try to increase your faith, to make your faith stronger so it will work better for you? What is wrong with this idea?

_____

_____

_____

_____

Are there issues in your life that you think would require a miracle to solve? Do you have faith God can do it? Why or why not?

_____

_____

_____

Is there someone you need to forgive for something? Something that you can't forgive in your own strength? How can God help you?

_____

_____

_____

_____

The Dangers of Respectability

Zacchaeus stood up and said to the Lord, "Look, Lord! Here and now I give half of my possessions to the poor, and if I have cheated anybody out of anything, I will pay back four times the amount." Jesus said to him, "Today salvation has come to this house, because this man, too, is a son of Abraham."

Luke 19:8–9 NIV

The Big Picture

The streets of Jericho were jammed with people trying to get a look at Jesus, trying to hear what he would say next, watching for what he would do next. A tax collector named Zacchaeus was there in the crowd, a little runt of a guy, so jostled and bumped that he couldn't see a thing. Finally, he broke free of the crowd; running ahead, he climbed a sycamore tree where he could see Jesus when he passed by.

Any grown man who perches up in a tree is exposing himself to ridicule. But in the case of Zacchaeus, the stakes were even higher than usual. He was already an object of loathing in Jericho. He was a Jew whose job was to collect taxes from his fellow Jews on behalf of their hated Roman rulers. In the process, he had become a rich man by cheating his countrymen. So Zacchaeus would have had good reason to lie low instead of climbing a tree where all of Jericho could see him.

When Jesus stopped at Zacchaeus's sycamore tree, no doubt the crowd thought the thieving little tax collector was about to get what he deserved. *So typical*, they might have thought, *there's Zacchaeus trying to get one more unfair advantage, running ahead, climbing a tree instead of staying down here on the ground like the rest of us. He doesn't even care that he looks like a fool. But this Jesus is a prophet. He won't be taken in by that little sneak.*

The crowd was astonished by the words Jesus spoke: "Zacchaeus, make haste and come down, for today I must stay at your house" (Luke 19:5 NKJV). What?! Most people in that crowd would have been thrilled to have the Prophet over for dinner. And Jesus went and bestowed that honor on a man like Zacchaeus?

Jesus' concern for Zacchaeus changed the little tax collector on the spot. The greedy, thieving Zacchaeus vowed to give half his goods to the poor, and he further vowed to pay back anything he had stolen times four. "Today salvation has come to this house," Jesus said. He came to "seek and to save what was lost" (19:10 NIV), and nobody needed to be saved from himself more than Zacchaeus did.

God has called us to despise evil, but he's never called us to despise the evildoer.

Max Lucado

Have you ever given much thought to the respectable people in this story? When you hear about the Zacchaeus story, you usually hear about the incredible change in Zacchaeus. The heart of a thief was totally transformed. But look how the "respectability" of the respectable people kept them from seeing the point. They weren't happy to see Jesus giving special attention to Zacchaeus: "He has gone to be a guest with a man who is a sinner" (19:7 NKJV).

Jesus didn't care about respectability. He came to those who needed him—the sinners, the sick, the poor, the socially unacceptable. He didn't care that Zacchaeus was a social outcast. Jesus saw a man willing to climb a tree to get a look at the Savior. He saw a man who wanted hope, who wanted something more than material wealth. Jesus came to change the hearts of sinners. And he didn't mind going against what the respectable people thought he should do in order to obey what God had given him to do.

> *The scope of who it is that God means to invite to the feast, you see, is not ours to define. We are not put in charge of the guest list.*
>
> Don C. Skinner

Have you known a genuinely rotten person whose heart was changed by the love of Jesus? It ought to be a source of great joy and celebration. But a lot of times it's just the opposite. The "respectable" people may not say it out loud, but they're thinking, *Wait a minute. This whole time I've been working my behind off to be good, he's been a back-stabbing jerk. How does he get off so easy?* Or sometimes the respectable people just whisper, "It'll never last. She's acting all righteous now, but you just wait. . . ."

It's easy to get excited about God's grace when it's extended to you or to somebody you like. But a Christlike heart rejoices just as much to see God's grace at work in the lives of hardened sinners. It's not your job to judge others, much less to decide what punishment God ought to dish out to them. You can always find somebody whose sins are more spectacular than yours, but remember, you need God's grace just as much as that person does. Jesus didn't come to congratulate people on their respectability. He came to change lives. Thank God for that!

Do not judge, so that you won't be judged.
Matthew 7:1 HCSB

Brennan Manning's book *The Ragamuffin Gospel* is a good reminder that the Gospel is not about respectability, but acknowledging your need. Here's how he sums up his book's message:

"The Ragamuffin Gospel was written for the bedraggled, beat-up, and burnt-out.

"It is for the sorely burdened who are still shifting the heavy suitcase from one hand to the other. . . .

"It is for inconsistent, unsteady disciples whose cheese is falling off their cracker.

"It is for poor, weak, sinful men and women with hereditary faults and limited talents."

In *Blue Like Jazz*, Donald Miller talks about what an incredible experience it was when he gave up his judgmental attitude toward other people:

"I was set free. I was free to love. I didn't have to discipline anybody, I didn't have to judge anybody, I could treat everybody as though they were my best friend, as though they were rock stars or famous poets, as though they were amazing, and to me they became amazing."

Zooming **In**

The Roman government forced the Jews to pay a large annual sum known as a tribute. That's what tax gatherers like Zacchaeus were collecting. Tax gatherers made extra money (sometimes a lot of it) by collecting more money than the Romans actually required and keeping the extra for themselves. No wonder they were so unpopular!

In the Jewish dietary laws, certain foods are considered unclean and therefore not to be eaten. Pork is the most well-known example. Certain "sinners" were considered unclean as well, and eating with them or entering their houses was forbidden. Tax collectors like Zacchaeus were near the top of the list of unclean people.

It's tough learning to see other people the way Jesus sees them. It's easier to sit in judgment than to really love somebody. But God makes it clear: none of us have any room to judge anybody else. Everybody is in need of God's grace, the respectable as well as the not-so-respectable.

Through the
Eyes of
Your Heart

What would you say is the modern equivalent of a tax collector? Is there some group of people that you have a prejudice toward—either consciously or unconsciously?

_____

_____

_____

Since the Bible is so clear that the gospel Is for sinners, do you think Christians are hung up on respectability? Explain.

_____

_____

_____

What can you do to look beyond the usual—the respectable—and touch those who seem to be beyond the reach of the gospel?

_____

_____

_____

_____

Freedom's Fruit

The fruit of the Spirit is love, joy, peace, patience, kindness, goodness, faithfulness, gentleness, self-control; against such things there is no law.

Galatians 5:22–23 ESV

The
Big Picture

The news from Galatia wasn't good. When Paul had visited the Galatian church, the people there responded to his message of freedom: Believers were free from the religious rules by which the Jewish people had sought to deserve God's favor. No more dietary laws. No more animal sacrifices. Even circumcision, the covenant sign that had always distinguished God's people from the rest of the world, was no longer necessary.

But when Paul left the Galatians to continue his missionary journeys, the Judaizers—men who taught that Christians had to follow Jewish laws—went to work on them. These false teachers convinced the Galatian people to give up the gospel freedom that Paul had preached. God's salvation couldn't come simply through grace and faith, the Judaizers taught. Grace and faith were fine as far as they went, the Judaizers said, but you must not forget about all those Jewish laws. The Judaizers expected even the Gentiles—non-Jews—who had joined the Galatian church to take on Jewish customs. They expected the Gentile men to be circumcised—no small demand in a world without anesthesia.

Paul had tangled with the Judaizers before. In fact, once in Antioch he had gotten in Peter's face when he found out that Peter had not been eating with the Gentile Christians when the Judaizers were around. So when Paul got word that his friends in Galatia had been listening to the Judaizers, he sat down to write an angry letter. That letter is now known as the book of Galatians in the New Testament.

"I am amazed that you are so quickly deserting Him who called you by the grace of Christ, for a different gospel," he wrote (Galatians 1:6 NASB). The Galatians had made themselves voluntary slaves, had taken on the chains that Jesus had released them from. The Judaizers were teaching that without the Jewish rules, people would start going berserk. But Paul addressed that point near the end of his letter. Believers must not use their freedom to indulge their worst desires. If you are walking by the Spirit, you won't fulfill the lusts of the flesh.

You've probably heard of the fruit of the Spirit: love, joy, peace, patience, kindness, goodness, faithfulness, gentleness, and self-control. No law, no rules or regulations, can give you that. You can become that kind of person only if you learn to rely on the Spirit instead of the rules.

It is the laden bough that hangs low, and the most fruitful Christian who is the most humble.

Author Unknown

You sometimes hear the phrase "fruits of the Spirit"—fruits, plural. But the Bible actually says "fruit of the Spirit"—fruit, singular. Maybe it's not a big thing, but that little distinction does point out the fact that the fruit of the Spirit is a package deal, not a salad bar. You don't say, "I'll take joy and peace, but no gentleness or self-control for me today, thanks."

The fruit of the Spirit is about a new heart. The old heart produces jealousy, anger, selfishness, contentiousness. Impose whatever rules you want to—you might even succeed in suppressing that fruit for a while—but ultimately the old heart is going to bear the old kind of fruit. The new, Spirit-led heart produces a whole different kind of fruit. It wants different things. Sure, you're going to slip up, do the wrong thing from time to time. But that won't be what characterizes your life. When you walk in the Spirit, as Paul puts it, you won't want to fulfill the desires of the flesh. If you're walking in the Spirit, your life will exhibit *all* the fruit of the Spirit. That's because all of your life—everything you do—is motivated by a new heart.

> *Now the Lord is the Spirit; and where the Spirit of the Lord is, there is liberty.*
>
> 2 Corinthians 3:17 NKJV

People react to rules in different ways. For some people, rules produce rebellion. "Who says I can't walk in the grass? I'll show them." For other people, rules are a source of security. "Just tell me what I need to do. Let me know what's expected of me."

Apply It
to Your Life

But life is complicated. You can't make up enough rules to deal with every situation in life. And what if there were that many rules? Would you really want to live that way? Jesus summed up the whole law of God in two sentences: "Love the Lord your God with all your heart and with all your soul and with all your strength and with all your mind. . . . Love your neighbor as yourself" (Luke 10:27 NIV). If you get that down—if you live that way—you'll be exhibiting the fruit of the Spirit. You can't get that from a rule book or a code of conduct. You can't do it in your own strength. Trust in your own ability to produce love, joy, peace, patience, kindness, goodness, faithfulness, gentleness, and self-control, and you're headed for burnout. That's why it's called the fruit of the *Spirit*. It's the Spirit that bears the fruit, not you. You have to trust the Spirit.

If you really love God with all your heart, soul, mind and strength and want whatever God wants for your life, you can do anything you please because you please to do what God wants you to do and not what God doesn't want for you to do.

J. David Hoke

How Others
See It

Judaizers may not be a problem in the Church any more, but there are still plenty of Christians who are suspicious of true Christian freedom. Charles Swindoll calls them "grace killers":

"They kill freedom, spontaneity, and creativity; they kill joy as well as productivity. They kill with their words and their pens and their looks. They kill with their attitudes far more often than their behavior. . . . The amazing thing is that they get away with it, day in and day out, without being confronted or exposed."

To exhibit the fruit of the Spirit is to be conformed to the image of Christ. So what is Paul getting at in this passage, freedom or conformity? Rick Warren addresses that issue in *The Purpose Driven Life*:

"God's ultimate goal for your life is not comfort, but character development. He wants you to grow spiritually and become like Christ. Becoming like Christ does not mean losing your personality or becoming a mindless clone. God created your uniqueness, so he certainly doesn't want to destroy it. Christlikeness is all about transforming your character, not your personality."

Zooming In

Beyond the theological dispute, the Judaizers' fight with Paul had an additional, personal element. In order to undermine Paul's authority, the Judaizers claimed that he wasn't a genuine apostle since he wasn't one of the original twelve apostles. Throughout his New Testament letters, Paul asserts his status as an apostle, at least partly in response to the Judaizers' attacks.

Because of its very clear statements about grace and faith (again, in response to the Judaizers' influence in Galatia), the book of Galatians was a favorite book of the Protestant reformers who spoke out against the abuses of the medieval church. Martin Luther loved Galatians so much, he called it his wife!

According to the teaching of Jesus, you know a tree by the kind of fruit it bears. The fruit of the Spirit is key to knowing where you stand in your Christian walk. Now is a good time to examine the fruit that is borne in your life.

Through the
Eyes of
Your Heart

Galatians 5:19–21 lists the works of the flesh, followed by the fruit of the Spirit. Read over those two lists. Which one more closely describes the fruit produced in your life?

_____

_____

_____

How have your desires changed over the past few years? What do you now want out of life that you didn't want before? Or what did you used to want that you now don't care about? Do you see evidence of growth in the fruit of the Spirit?

_____

_____

_____

In Galatians 5 Paul talks about the flesh and the Spirit opposing each other, causing you to do things you don't really want to do. How do you experience this phenomenon in your life?

_____

_____

_____

Your Brother's Keeper

Cain said to his brother Abel, "Let's go out to the field." And while they were in the field, Cain attacked his brother Abel and killed him. Then the LORD said to Cain, "Where is your brother Abel?"

"I don't know," he replied. "Am I my brother's keeper?"

Genesis 4:8–9 NIV

The Big Picture

A petty jealousy. A sibling rivalry. The world's first murder. Cain and Abel were the sons of Adam and Eve. Cain, the older brother, was a farmer. Abel was a shepherd. Both men brought an offering to God that was appropriate to his line of work: Cain brought some of the crops he had grown, and Abel brought one of the sheep he had raised. But God only accepted Abel's offering. Cain's offering he rejected. It's not that farm produce was an inappropriate offering; after all, God instituted the grain offering as well as animal sacrifice. Obviously there was something amiss in Cain's attitude. God asked, "If you do well, will you not be accepted? And if you do not do well, sin lies at the door. And its desire is for you, but you should rule over it" (Genesis 4:7 NKJV).

The sacrifice that Cain offered was obviously an empty ritual, not a reflection of any true devotion. Cain, however, refused to take responsibility for his attitude problem. Rather than submitting to God—rather than ruling over the sin that was crouching at his door—Cain took out his frustration on his younger brother. He killed Abel, as if he believed it to be Abel's fault that God rejected Cain's sacrifice.

God confronted Cain with what he had done: "Where is Abel your brother?" Cain still refused to take responsibility. He began with a flat-out lie: "I don't know." Then he added a bit of smart-aleck sarcasm: "Am I my brother's keeper?" In other words, "What do I look like, a babysitter?"

Not the right answer. The first family had a habit of trying to put one over on God. After Adam and Eve ate the fruit of the forbidden tree, they tried to hide from the God who sees everything. They seemed unclear on the concept of God's omniscience—his all-knowing power. Cain had the same problem. He apparently didn't understand that God already knew the answer to the question he asked. God only asked it to give Cain one more chance to take responsibility for his action. Cain chose to play dumb instead. And rather than being ruled by God, rather than ruling over his sin, he chose to let himself be ruled by his own worst tendencies.

It is well to remember that the entire universe, with one trifling exception, is composed of others.

John Andrew Holmes

"Am I my brother's keeper?" Cain thought he was asking a rhetorical question—a question so obvious that it didn't require an answer. "Duh," you can almost hear him say. "It's not my job to keep up with him." What Cain didn't understand was that he *was* his brother's keeper. He *did* have a responsibility to his brother.

Jesus taught that murder starts in the heart. "You have heard that it was said to those of old, 'You shall not murder.' . . . But I say to you that whoever is angry with his brother without a cause shall be in danger of the judgment" (Matthew 5:21–22 NKJV). You almost wonder if Jesus had Cain in mind when he made that comment.

Cain's sarcastic comment wasn't an isolated thing. It was directly related to everything else that happened in this story. Cain lived in his own little world. He never let responsibilities to God or to anybody else interfere with his self-absorption. When God didn't accept Cain's sacrifice, that was Cain's problem, and Cain had it in his power to take care of it. Instead, he took out his anger on his brother. If Cain had only asked himself, "Am I my brother's keeper?"—not as a sarcastic rhetorical question, but as a real question—everything might have been different.

> *Do nothing from selfishness or empty conceit, but with humility of mind regard one another as more important than yourselves.*
>
> Philippians 2:3 NASB

It's human nature to put yourself first. But God calls you to look out for others, too. Are you your brother's keeper? Yes, you are. That doesn't mean you have to bear the weight of the world on your shoulders, nor does it mean you have to let yourself be controlled by manipulative people. It does mean you need to step outside your own little world and think about other people.

Here's one of the great ironies of human nature: the deeper you get into your own selfishness, the less you are actually able to look out for yourself. Think about Cain; if only he had stepped out of his self-absorption long enough to wonder why God rejected his offering, he could have made things right. Instead, he got angry and let hatred lead him down a terrible path.

God told Cain to rule over his own sinful nature. He tells you the same thing. Selfish habits make it harder and harder to rule over your own worst tendencies. But when you're loving other people—when you remember that you *are* your brother's keeper—you grow in the self-control that keeps you on the road to genuine happiness.

He who rules within himself and rules passions, desires, and fears is more than a king.

John Milton

You've heard the saying "Love is blind." But as the story of Cain shows, love isn't nearly as blind as hatred and selfishness. Here is Eugene Peterson's observation in *Where the Heart Is*:

"It is hate that is blind. It is habit, condescension, cynicism that are blind. Love opens eyes. Love enables the eyes to see what has been there all along but was overlooked in haste or indifference. Love corrects astigmatism so that what was distorted in selfishness is now perceived accurately and appreciatively."

C. S. Lewis's *Screwtape Letters* are imaginary letters from one devil to the other on the subject of how best to corrupt the soul of a new Christian. Its upside-down look at things (God is always referred to as "The Enemy") provides a lot of insight into how we human beings interact with the spiritual world. Here's what Screwtape had to say about self-forgetfulness:

"When [God] speaks of their losing their selves, He means only abandoning the clamour of self-will; once they have done that, He really gives them back all their personality, and boasts (I am afraid, sincerely) that when they are wholly His they will be more themselves than ever."

Zooming **In**

When people use the phrase "the Land of Nod," they're usually referring to nodding off to sleep. However, the phrase originally had nothing to do with peaceful sleep. It originated in Cain's story. After Cain murdered Abel, God banished him, and he settled east of Eden, in a place called the land of Nod.

Adam and Eve had other children besides Cain and Abel. The only one named in Genesis is Seth. His name means "seed" in Hebrew. It was an appropriate name, for from the seed of Seth (not from Cain) grew the lineage that gave rise to the nation of Israel, and eventually to Jesus himself.

Yes, you have responsibilities to other people, not to mention responsibilities to God. But keep this one thing in mind: learning to forget about yourself doesn't mean losing yourself or giving up your happiness. No, selflessness is actually the shortcut to happiness. What greater freedom than being free from self-absorption?

Reflect on the selflessness of Jesus. Though he had in his person all the glory of God, he emptied it all out and became a human being—and a very humble one at that. How does that fact affect your view of yourself and your place in the world?

_____

_____

Everybody is guilty of selfishness somewhere in his or her life. What are the selfish spots that you need to work on? How can you begin to make progress in those areas?

_____

_____

_____

No doubt you exhibit selflessness, too. How can you build on those good things, so that selflessness can begin taking over all your interactions with others?

_____

_____

_____

A Boat with No Rudder?

So make yourself an ark of cypress wood; make rooms in it and coat it with pitch inside and out. This is how you are to build it: The ark is to be 450 feet long, 75 feet wide and 45 feet high. Make a roof for it and finish the ark to within 18 inches of the top. Put a door in the side of the ark and make lower, middle and upper decks.

Genesis 6:14–16 NIV

The Big Picture

Noah was a very old man when he heard the voice of God: "Make yourself an ark of cypress wood." That word *ark*, by the way, doesn't mean "boat." An ark is a chest or a box. And Noah's was the mother of all arks—the length of one and a half football fields, half the width of a football field, and about four stories high! It would have taken Noah and his three sons years to build the thing. And there would have been no way to do it in secret. The neighbors would have surely noticed that he was involved in an enormous construction project.

"What are you building, Noah?"

"An ark."

"That's the biggest ark I've ever seen. What are you going to do with it?"

"My family and I are going to float in it."

The neighbor looks at the ark again. *"How do you plan to get that thing to the water?"*

"I won't have to. The water's going to come to me. God is so frustrated with the wickedness of the human race that he's sending a flood to destroy everyone. Only my family will be spared, in this ark."

The neighbor suspects the old man is losing it. Who has ever heard of such a flood? There's not a cloud in the sky. And he's not sure he appreciates Noah's suggestion that he's so wicked he deserves to be washed away. Still, he can't help egging Noah on a little. "This ark of yours is a little big for a family of eight, isn't it? If you're concerned about a flood, why don't you just get a big boat?"

"Well, actually it won't be just my family in the ark. We're taking a mating pair of every kind of animal with us—seven each of the clean animals."

You can imagine that Noah and his family were subject to more than their share of ridicule.

But when the Flood came, Noah and his family were safe, spared thanks to the mercy of God, who looked on them with favor. It's an amazing thing to think about: amid all that destruction and death, all the life left on the earth floated on the surface of the water in that dark, loud, smelly ark, protected by the same hand that had opened the floodgates. Noah's faith and God's faithfulness salvaged life on earth.

Don't be intimidated. Remember, the Ark was built by amateurs; the Titanic, by professionals.

Author Unknown

Think of the pictures you've seen of Noah's ark. It's usually depicted as a big, bulky boat, isn't it? In many pictures, the front of the ark sharpens to a nice prow for cutting through the water. Sometimes, especially in children's books, there's even a steering wheel with Noah in a yellow rain slicker steering his ship to safety while a giraffe, its head sticking through an upstairs window, looks down on him.

But the ark was more like a big chest than a boat. In other words, it was good for containing and protecting, but there would have been no way any person could steer it. All Noah and his family could do was ride out the storm and place their trust in God. Not only was there no steering mechanism, there apparently wasn't even a mechanism for closing the door. The Bible specifies that once the rains started, Noah and his family boarded the ark and God shut them in. They were totally at God's mercy. After years and years of hard work and faithful obedience, ultimately they had to surrender their efforts and trust in the God who had promised to save them.

> The human mind plans the way, but the LORD directs the steps.
>
> Proverbs 16:9 NRSV

There are times in your life when there's nothing left for you to do but trust in God. You've done
all you can do—or maybe you haven't—but some-

Apply It
to Your Life

times life gets too intense for you to make it on
your own. Noah and his sons worked very hard
for a very long time; they no doubt put up with a
lot of ridicule, allowing themselves to look like
fools in the eyes of the world. But even that didn't make them responsible for
their own destiny. They had to rely on God.

Living the Christian life means striking a balance between doing your job
and letting God do his. When you are obedient to God, you build your life into
an ark of safety—a life that's tight enough to float on top of the water, solid
enough to withstand the wind and waves without sinking. But no matter how
obedient you are, how solid your life is, it's still God who's steering the ship.
And when life is overwhelming, you know that even if you can't keep your
hand on the tiller, God has everything under control. Salvation belongs to
God, not you. And that's a good thing.

*The Ark ended up on Ararat not because of chance winds,
but because God controlled Noah's salvation—Noah just
had to follow God's plan to build the Ark.*

John Mackay

In a "Daily Wisdom" devotion at www.gospelcom.net, Carl Holmes speculates on Noah's reaction to God's surprising blueprint for the ark:

"Why did God not put a rudder on the ark? Can you imagine Noah saying, 'Umm, God, I have a question. Do You think we can put a rudder on this thing?' Instead, Noah's reaction was, 'Yes, God; I will do as You command. I will get out of my comfort zone, I will do what You have asked me to do and I will do Your will.'"

As Os Hillman points out, the relationship between God and Noah was a covenant; Noah had his part to play, and God had his:

"Noah did not have to invent the ark; God gave him the plans—in specific dimensional detail. He did not have to gather the animals—God led them into the ark. God even closed the door when they all came on board. . . . The covenant provided all Noah needed to complete his mission in life."

Zooming **In**

In the Garden of Eden, the earth was watered not by rain, but by a mist that rose up from the ground (see Genesis 2:6). The account of Noah's flood hearkens back to the idea of water coming up from the ground, this time in an uncontrolled torrent: "all the fountains of the great deep burst open, and the floodgates of the sky were opened" (Genesis 7:11 NASB). It's as if God, seeing that the people of earth wanted to live free from his control, said, "Okay, I'll show you what happens when I release my control on the life-giving waters both below the earth and above it."

In a scene of chaos and destruction, Noah's ark was a haven of safety, steered not by Noah or his family, but by God himself. That's a picture of a life hidden in Christ. Spend some time reflecting on what the story of Noah has to do with your life.

Through the
Eyes of
Your Heart

Walking in faith means striking a balance between actively obeying and resting in God's work. What comes more easily for you—working or trusting? How can you strike a better balance?

The world can be a rough place to live when you're trying to please God. What changes do you need to make in order to have a life that's more solid and more watertight?

For centuries, Christian teachers have viewed Noah's ark as a picture of the church. How is the ark like the church?

Forward-Looking Gratitude

Then Jacob made a vow, saying, "If God will be with me and will keep me on this journey that I take, and will give me food to eat and garments to wear, and I return to my father's house in safety, then the LORD will be my God."

Genesis 28:20–21 NASB

The
Big Picture

Jacob was on the run from his brother Esau, and with good reason. Jacob had always been the tricky one, the clever one. Years before, he had outwitted Esau and convinced him to trade his birthright—the older brother's right of inheritance—for a pot of stew. But the last straw came when Jacob disguised himself as Esau to trick their aged, blind father Isaac into bestowing on him the blessing that was supposed to go to the older brother. Esau vowed to kill Jacob as soon as their father died, which wasn't very far away. There was no reason to doubt that Esau could or would do it. He was a big, brawny man and a hunter, so he was skilled at killing and accustomed to it. He may not have been as clever as Jacob, but Esau was definitely a man of action.

So it's easy to see why Jacob wasn't hanging around the house. Actually, his father sent him away for his own safety. Isaac may not have appreciated the trick Jacob played on him, but since both the birthright and the blessing had ended up with Jacob, he now represented Isaac's hopes for posterity. He packed Jacob off to the house of his brother-in-law Laban in Paddan-aram.

One night on the journey to his uncle's house, Jacob lay down on the ground to sleep, in a place called Beersheba. He used one of the stones of the place for a pillow. As he slept, he dreamed of a huge ladder, reaching from earth up to heaven, and angels were going up and down the ladder. Above it all was God, who spoke to Jacob and told him that he would give the land where he slept to Jacob and his descendants, and that his descendants would be vast in number and spread throughout the earth. More than that, they would be a blessing to all the earth.

When Jacob awoke from his dream, he was filled with a terrified joy. "This is the gate of heaven" (Genesis 28:17 NASB), he marveled. He took up the stone that he had used for a pillow and set it up as a pillar, a memorial to the promise God had made there. He called the place Bethel, then he made a vow: if God would keep him safe and bring him safely home, the Lord would be his God.

Jacob learned that when you are walking with the Lord any place becomes your resting place. Wherever you are Yahweh is there.

Wil Pounds

There are a couple of ways of looking at Jacob's vow. Some people view it as Jacob's trying to cut a deal with God: "Okay, God, that was a pretty good show. But if you want me to serve you as Lord, you've got to meet my needs first. Keep me safe, provide for me, return me to my father's house, and *then* you can be my God." A more positive view of Jacob's vow is this: "If God can do all this—keep me safe, meet my needs, bring me home—surely I can serve him as Lord."

Jacob's vision was truly awesome. No doubt the family had passed down stories of how God had spoken to Jacob's grandfather Abraham, how God promised to make a great nation of his descendants. Now Jacob had seen God for himself, had heard the promise made directly to *him*. He knew he was in the hands of a mighty God. God said, "I will not leave you until I have done what I have promised you" (Genesis 28:15 NASB). After what he had just seen, could Jacob really doubt that God would keep his promise? There was no other response but to say, "The LORD will be my God" (28:21 NASB).

See, God has come to save me. I will trust in him and not be afraid.

Isaiah 12:2 NLT

If you are in Christ, your life ought to be characterized by an attitude of gratitude. God has already filled your life with things to be thankful for. But for a Christian, there's also a forward-looking component to gratitude. The life of faith is a matter of being thankful for things that haven't happened yet.

How does that work? The promises of God are sure. He promises to work all things to the good of those who love him. He promises to give you abundant life. He promises to give you peace and rest. Some of his promises you have already experienced. Some are not yet fulfilled. But because God is always faithful, his future blessings are just as sure as past and present blessings. They may not seem so from a human, time-bound perspective, but they are.

Jacob's experience of God's presence made him say, "The Lord will be my God." As you look forward to adulthood, you can be just as certain of God's blessings as Jacob was. You don't have to wonder whether God will take care of you. You can say, "*Since* God is going to do great things, the Lord will be my God."

To see God is the promised goal of all our actions and the promised height of all our joys.

Saint Augustine

David Roper reflects on Jacob's life after the amazing experience at Bethel. God didn't promise an easy life for Jacob; he promised to be with him:

"Jacob had no idea what lay ahead. His years in Haran were brutal, painful years, filled with anxiety and grief, yet God proved to be as good as his word. He was with Jacob every step of the way. That's what rendered Jacob quiet and at ease despite the difficulties of those days."

John Piper's book *Future Grace* is about a gratitude that looks both backward and forward:

"With true gratitude there is such a delight in the worth of God's past grace, that we are driven on to experience more and more of it in the future. . . . [This] is done by transforming gratitude into faith as it turns from contemplating the pleasures of past grace and starts contemplating the promises of the future."

Zooming In

Jacob wasn't the only person to set up a stone to memorialize an important day. It seemed to be a common practice in Bible times. When the people of Israel crossed over the river Jordan to enter the Promised Land after forty years of wandering, Joshua commanded that twelve stones be set up in the river to commemorate the day the twelve tribes of Israel entered the land. The whole point was to be a conversation starter. When the Israelites' children asked what those twelve stones were doing in the river, their parents would have a chance to tell the story of God's deliverance.

The story of Jacob's vow at Bethel sheds light on what it means to trust in God and to submit to God's guidance and control. You probably won't have a spectacular vision like Jacob's, but the promises of God apply to you just as much as they applied to Jacob.

Jacob's commitment to God was based on his confidence in God's faithfulness. What is the basis of your confidence in God?

_____

_____

_____

In the above passage, John Piper talks about transforming backward-looking gratitude into future-looking hope. What blessings from the past give you hope for the future God has planned for you?

_____

_____

_____

What is it that you really hope for the future? How well do you think your hopes line up with God's plan for your life?

_____

_____

_____

_____

God Will Provide a Lamb

Isaac said, "[B]ut where is the lamb for the burnt offering?"
Abraham answered, "God himself will provide the lamb for the
burnt offering, my son." . . .

[H]e saw a ram caught by its horns. He went over and took the
ram and sacrificed it as a burnt offering instead of his son.

Genesis 22:7–8, 13 NIV

The **Big Picture**

Abraham had waited all his life for a child. God had promised long before to make Abraham's descendants into a great nation. But Abraham became a very old man, and Sarah became a very old woman, and still there were no children. When two messengers came to tell Sarah and Abraham that they would have a son within a year, Sarah laughed at the very idea. Who could blame her? She was ninety years old, for crying out loud. How could she have a baby?

But a year later, Sarah's mocking laughter had turned into the laughter of joy as she held baby Isaac. A ninety-year-old wife and a hundred-year-old husband were suddenly first-time parents! Can you imagine how much Abraham and Sarah doted on this miracle child, Isaac? Not only was he the only child of aged parents, but he represented the fulfillment of a promise they had cherished for decades. In Isaac lived Abraham's hope of becoming a great nation—a hope that had been sorely challenged in the many years since God first made the promise.

When Isaac got a little older, Abraham received a terrible command from God: "Take now your son, your only son, whom you love, Isaac, and go to the land of Moriah, and offer him there as a burnt offering" (Genesis 22:2 NASB). Sacrifice his beloved son, the gift of God, the very evidence of God's faithfulness?

It was an incredible test of obedience. But Abraham obeyed. He and his only son headed to the place appointed for the sacrifice. Isaac saw the wood, he saw the fire, he saw the knife, but he saw no animal for the sacrifice. "Where is the lamb?" he asked.

"God himself will provide the lamb," Abraham answered. But by the time he had built an altar, Abraham still had no lamb. He laid the wood on the altar. He laid the boy on the wood. He raised the knife, surely praying that God would intervene.

At the last moment, God did intervene. When he saw that Abraham wouldn't even withhold his only son, God ordered him to hold his hand. And in a nearby thicket, Abraham noticed for the first time that there was a ram whose horns had gotten stuck. Just as Abraham said, God provided an animal for the sacrifice. And because Abraham passed the test, God renewed the promise to make a great nation of him.

Abraham gave up everything he owned and in doing so, acquired everything God had for him.

Benji Kelley

Abraham demonstrated incredible obedience in this episode. Isaac was a miraculous gift from God, the source of great joy to his father. But Abraham didn't value the gift more than the Giver. As painful as obedience was, Abraham knew to obey. "God himself will provide the lamb," he said. And God did provide.

Ultimately, this story is about God's faithfulness more than Abraham's. If you read the story in Genesis 22, you'll notice something unusual about God's language. Three times God refers to Abraham's son Isaac, and each time he uses the phrase "your son, your only son." At first it looks as if God is taking Abraham's pain and rubbing it in: sacrifice "your son, your only son, whom you love" (Genesis 22:2 NASB). Isn't this hard enough for Abraham already, without having to be reminded that Isaac is his only son?

Why did God use this language so insistently? Surely he was drawing attention to the fact that he would himself sacrifice his Son, his only Son Jesus. And that time there would be no last-minute rescue. God provided a lamb to die in the place of Isaac. He also provided the Lamb of God to die in your place.

> *For God loved the world in this way: He gave His One and Only Son, so that everyone who believes in Him will not perish but have eternal life.*
>
> John 3:16 HCSB

If you find the story of Abraham and Isaac to be confusing, that's okay. God's testing of Abraham does appear to be cruel. Even though you don't have kids yet, you can imagine just how awful it would be to face what Abraham faced—to have to choose between obeying God and holding on to the beloved child you had waited so long for. And if you think it was terrifying for Abraham, think what it would have been like for the boy Isaac. Sure, everything worked out, and a ram miraculously appeared in the nick of time, but the trauma leading up to it!

The thing that keeps God's test from being a cruel trick is the fact that God wasn't asking Abraham to do anything he wouldn't do himself. The sin of the world is an ugly business, and the solution—a Father sacrificing his Son, his only Son—is terrible to think about. The story of Abraham and Isaac is *supposed* to make you queasy. "God loved the world in this way: He gave His One and Only Son . . ." Think that's just abstract, spiritual talk? The story of Abraham and Isaac gives you a better sense of what that familiar verse really means.

You and I were in Isaac's terrible predicament, with no hope of release or victory, until God sent Jesus to take our place, to suffer for our sins, and to die on our behalf.

Rod Benson

In her book *When I Lay My Isaac Down*, Carol Kent reflects on what it meant for Abraham to sacrifice his son:

"At that moment he relinquished his own desires, dreams, plans, and hopes for his Isaac's future and made the sacrifice an act of worship to the God he trusted with a confidence so strong that even if God allowed his son to die, Abraham knew God could raise him from the dead."

God's command to sacrifice Isaac seems to contradict his earlier promises to Abraham. Why doesn't the Bible say more about Abraham's struggle with this contradiction? In his commentary on the book of Hebrews, Frederick Fyvie Bruce makes an interesting point:

"The impression which we get from the biblical narrative is that Abraham treated it as God's problem. It was for God, and not for Abraham, to reconcile his promise and his command. So, when the command was given, Abraham promptly set out obeying it; his own duty was clear; and God could safely be trusted to discharge *his* responsibility in the matter."

Zooming **In**

According to tradition, the mountain (Moriah) where Abraham laid Isaac on the altar was the same hill where King Solomon built the temple in Jerusalem. Abraham's sacrifice would be the first of many performed by God's people on that hill. Now the Dome of the Rock, an important Muslim holy place, stands there.

Child sacrifice was practiced in the worship of various pagan gods in the ancient Middle East. The Ammonite god Moloch, or Molech, is the most well-known of the gods to whom children were sacrificed. During one period of especially rampant idolatry, even the Hebrews built an altar to Molech and sacrificed their children.

The story of Abraham and Isaac at Mount Moriah has given believers a lot to think about for millennia. It's not the sort of story that lends itself to easy answers. You might want to spend some time processing this very difficult passage of Scripture.

Through the
Eyes of
Your Heart

Are there things in your life that you wouldn't be able to sacrifice if God asked you to? What makes it so hard to let go?

_____

_____

_____

_____

There are times in your life when the promises of God don't seem to square up with what you can see God doing. How do you reconcile that apparent contradiction when you experience it?

_____

_____

_____

Do you think it would have been harder to do what Abraham did, or what Isaac did in this story? Why?

_____

_____

_____

_____

Going Public

Behold, when we come into the land, you shall tie this scarlet cord in the window through which you let us down, and you shall gather into your house your father and mother, your brothers, and all your father's household.

Joshua 2:18 ESV

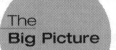

The Big Picture

When the Israelites conquered the Promised Land, their first major military objective was the great walled city of Jericho. While they were planning their attack, they sent two spies to enter the city and scope it out.

The two spies found lodging at the house of a prostitute named Rahab. Her house was built into the city walls with a window to the outside—perfect for a quick getaway, even if the city gates were closed. No doubt that's one reason the spies chose Rahab's house for their base of operations.

The people of Jericho noticed the suspicious strangers. Somebody told the king of Jericho that there were Israelite spies in the city, and they told him where to find them. The king sent word to Rahab to hand over the men. But Rahab had already hidden them on the roof of her house. She lied to the king's men. Yes, she said, two men had come to her house, but she didn't know where they came from. They left before the city gates closed at dark. The soldiers could still catch them out on the plain if they hurried.

Rahab could see the writing on the wall. She, like the rest of Jericho, had heard about the great things God had done for the Israelites. She knew how God had split the Red Sea, and they had walked safely out of Egypt. She knew about their amazing military victory over the Amorites. She knew the Israelites' God was God over heaven and earth. That's why she chose to help the spies. The rest of Jericho had lost heart—"our hearts melted" (Joshua 2:11 NASB), Rahab told the spies—but Rahab took action. She threw in her lot with the one true God.

When the coast was clear, Rahab sent the men through the outside window. But before she did, she made them promise to repay her kindness by sparing her and her family when the invasion came. The Israelites agreed to her request. They told her to hang a red cord out the window they escaped from so the Israelites would know which house to spare.

When the attack came, the walls of Jericho fell flat. But one house stood, its inhabitants safe amid the destruction. A red cord hung from its window.

Rahab did not let her sinful past keep her from laying hold of the treasures of God's grace. She seized the new role God had for her among His people.

Cheryl Ford

Take a closer look at the red cord hanging from Rahab's window. It's a public sign of a private choice. Rahab was forced to choose between death and life. When you put it in those terms, it seems like an easy choice: who wouldn't choose life? But the decision is almost never that easy. In Rahab's case, choosing life meant being totally out of step with her society. Think about what Rahab's life was like in the days between the spies' promise and the actual invasion. She was still in Jericho, living among the people she had known all her life, but she was no longer one of them. She had become an Israelite stranded in enemy territory, waiting to be joined to her true people.

It's the sort of thing she may have preferred to keep to herself. But the Israelite spies didn't leave her that option. Her salvation depended on her going public. That red cord was there for everyone to see. Surely Rahab thought twice before hanging that red cord out her window. There was a definite risk of her townspeople knowing she had gone to the other side. But how much greater the risk of having the cord hidden when the invasion came!

> If we stick it out with [Jesus], we'll rule with him; if we turn our backs on him, he'll turn his back on us.
>
> 2 Timothy 2:12 MSG

If you are living for Christ, you are like Rahab, living between the promise and the invasion. You're out of step with your society. That's the way it's supposed to be. You're called not to be conformed to the world around you, but to be transformed into a new person. To be a Christian is to have your true citizenship in another king-

dom from the one where you physically live. That can make you feel like a weirdo when everybody else seems to be doing fine without God, living for themselves and generally having a good time.

You may be tempted to hide the fact that you've gone over to the other side. It's easier just to blend in. But if you have truly been changed on the inside, you will show it on the outside. You have to go public, hang out the red cord. Jesus said, "Whoever denies Me before men, I will also deny him before My Father who is in heaven" (Matthew 10:33 NASB). That ought to get your attention. The invasion is coming. The kingdoms of earth will become the kingdoms of God. You don't want to be caught hiding your true citizenship when the King returns.

Our inner life of faith ought to be reflected in an outward life of faithfulness and good works.

John MacArthur

Ann Spangler and Jean E. Syswerda have a section on Rahab in their devotional book, *Women of the Bible*:

"Rahab's story is a dramatic one. It shows us that God's grace accepts no boundaries. The red cord that saved Rahab and her family reminds us of the red blood of Jesus, who still saves us today. . . . Rahab put her faith in the God of Israel and was not disappointed."

In his commentary on the book of Hebrews, R. Kent Hughes speculates on the origins of Rahab's faith, which perhaps was sparked by traveling merchants who brought news of the Israelites who had been wandering in the wilderness:

"Rahab heard that there was only one God, Jehovah. She heard bits and snatches about Israel's destiny. She heard, perhaps derisively, of the nation's high ethical and moral code. Perhaps she had become disillusioned with the culture around her. . . . She had seen life at its worst. All of this together made her open to truth and faith."

Zooming **In**

Rahab went on to be an important figure in biblical history. She entered Israelite society, married an Israelite man named Salmon, and was the great-great-grandmother of King David. Which means that this former heathen prostitute turned out to be an ancestor of the Messiah. Who would have predicted such a thing when the spies first showed up at Rahab's door?

Archaeologists have located the ancient site of Jericho. Evidence shows that the city fell quickly, as the Bible indicated, and not as the result of a slow starvation siege, which would have been more common in that era. Archaeologists also discovered that Jericho had two concentric walls, not one wall. Houses (including Rahab's, perhaps?) stood between the two walls.

What an incredible story: Rahab's faith seems to come out of nowhere. But it totally changes her life, inside and out. There's plenty in this ancient story that makes a difference in your life today.

Through the
Eyes of
Your Heart

 In what ways do you experience being "out of step with your society"?

....

....

_____

_____

 What are the dangers of "hanging out the red cord" in your life?

....

....

_____

_____

 What are the dangers of not "hanging out the red cord"?

....

_____

....

....

A Strong Man's Weakness

With men hidden in the room, she called to him, "Samson, the Philistines are upon you!" But he snapped the thongs.... Then Delilah said to Samson, "You have made a fool of me; you lied to me. Come now, tell me how you can be tied."

Judges 16:9–10 NIV

The Big Picture

Samson is one of those people in the Bible who's just hard to figure out. How could one guy—especially a guy who enjoyed as many blessings and advantages as Samson—be so stupid? He was like the Incredible Hulk without the green skin. When it came to fighting the Philistines, he was an unstoppable force. But for all his physical strength, Samson had some serious weaknesses. He liked Philistine women, who were supposed to be off-limits for a God-fearing Israelite. That weakness, combined with excessive pride in his own abilities, spelled big trouble for Samson.

Samson fell in love with a Philistine woman named Delilah, and she was trouble. The Philistine leaders convinced Delilah to get Samson to tell her the secret of his strength, so they could overpower him. At first Samson had sense enough not to tell her. He made up a story about how he would be just like any other man if he were tied with seven new bowstrings. The next time he went to sleep, he awoke to find he had been tied with seven new cords, and the house was full of Philistines waiting to ambush him.

take a **CLOSER** look for teens

There was no harm done, but wouldn't you think that would be Samson's first clue that he was in an unhealthy relationship? His girlfriend had obviously betrayed him. Yet she acted as if he were the one who had let her down. Delilah begged and pouted, so Samson gave her another answer—another lie. Samson told her that if his hair were woven into a loom, he would lose his strength. The results were predictable. Samson woke up with his hair woven in Delilah's loom, and the place was crawling with Philistine agents.

The fourth time, Delilah broke Samson. In spite of what he had seen, he told her the true story of his strength: it was in his hair, which had never been cut. Cut his hair, and he would be like any other man. Samson woke up with his head shaved. Philistine men were there to arrest him. And he was enslaved by the very people he had terrorized his whole life. The Spirit of God finally left him, returning only for one spectacular moment at the very end of his life, when he prayed for strength to pull a Philistine temple down on top of his enemies and himself.

What is strength without a double share of wisdom?

John Milton

Samson had taken a vow never to cut his hair. His strength wasn't exactly in his hair, but rather in the vow he had taken to remain set apart for God's service. The hair was just the outward symbol of that vow. By allowing Delilah to cut his hair, he was breaking his deal with God and forfeiting the particular blessing (strength) that came with his vow. Why would Samson do such a thing? Perhaps because he had come to believe his strength was his own, inseparable from himself, rather than a gift from God.

Samson was a thrill seeker. He spent his whole life getting closer to the edge and enjoying the thrill of coming out unscathed. His amazing exploits had made him a major celebrity, and he liked it that way. The problem was that Samson started believing his own press clippings. He came to believe that he really was unstoppable. He forgot that all that power, all that success, came from God, and he was supposed to use it to serve God, not to serve himself. Samson was stupid all right, but his real problem wasn't stupidity. It wasn't even a weakness for bad women. It was plain old pride.

> *Pride leads to destruction, and arrogance to downfall.*
>
> Proverbs 16:18 GNT

God has given you a unique set of gifts and talents, and he has given them for a unique purpose. But it's no easy thing to come to terms with your own gifts. On the one hand, you may find it hard to believe you actually have any real talents. You see talented people all around you, but you don't feel you measure up. If that's the case, you aren't just selling yourself short; you're selling God short, too.

On the other hand, maybe you do realize you've got talent—but then what? The challenge is to keep your talent in perspective: it is a gift from God, given to you for the purpose of serving him. The tricky part is that any gift that can be used to serve God can also be used to serve self. It feels good to receive the praise of others. As you get more confident in your abilities (and you should), there's always the danger of putting trust in your gifts rather than in the Giver. As you put your talents to good use, ask God for wisdom to balance humility with a confidence in his ability to do great things through you.

The heart of a man is revealed in temptation.
Dietrich Bonhoeffer

In *Big Dummies of the Bible*, Stephen M. Miller draws lessons from the lives of some of the most idiotic people in Scripture. And who's more idiotic than Samson?

"If we break one of God's laws, and do something we know is wrong, we might as well break our own arm. We hurt ourselves when we break God's rules. Those rules are there to protect us. It's like telling children not to touch the hot stove. Too often curiosity wins and fingers lose. The stakes are often higher for adults. Our curiosity, passion, or greed can win, but it can cost us jobs, relationships, and reputation."

In *Lessons from a Sheep Dog*, Phillip Keller discusses the same issues of freedom and self-gratification that led to Samson's downfall:

"Those who brag about being free seldom realize they are inexorably bound by their own destructive lifestyles. They are trapped in the toils of their own destructive decisions and desires. Nor can they be loosed except by the loving hands of the Good Shepherd."

Zooming In

The vow that forbade Samson to cut his hair was called a Nazirite vow. The Nazirite vow also forbade him from eating anything unclean or drinking wine or any other "strong drink." The word *Nazirite* means "separated." A person (man or woman) took a Nazirite vow in order to be specially devoted to God for a certain period of time. When the period of the vow was complete, the Nazirite was to shave his or her head and burn the hair on the sacrificial altar. Samson is the only person mentioned in the Bible who was a Nazirite for life.

The story of Samson is sobering: here's a guy who had every advantage, every opportunity to enjoy doing great things for God. But he got so wrapped up in himself that he missed out on all of that. But his mistakes are avoidable, if only you pay attention.

Through the
Eyes of
Your Heart

God gave you your unique set of talents and abilities; he intended them to be used for his glory. How can you use your gifts to serve God?

_____

_____

_____

_____

Samson looked a lot like one of the spoiled, self-indulgent celebrities you see on the magazines at the grocery checkout. How should a Christian respond to this culture's self-worship and celebrity worship?

_____

_____

_____

As Samson's story shows, when you give in to temptation in one area of life, you lose ground in other areas that you thought you had under control. What are the trouble spots in your life where you need to regain control?

_____

_____

_____

A Whirlwind Tour

As they were going along and talking, behold, there appeared a chariot of fire and horses of fire which separated the two of them. And Elijah went up by a whirlwind to heaven.

2 Kings 2:11 NASB

The Big Picture

Elijah was one of the greatest of Israel's prophets. He came to prominence just when the worship of the true God was in danger of disappearing from the kingdom of Israel. King Ahab had married the pagan princess Jezebel, and under her influence the worship of the false god Baal flourished. Israel was crawling with priests of Baal, and there were very few voices speaking for God. But Elijah courageously faced down both King Ahab and Queen Jezebel, not to mention all the priests of Baal.

Elijah was a country boy from an obscure village in backwater Gilead; he wasn't a sharp dresser by any means. One person described him as "a hairy man with a leather girdle bound about his loins" (2 Kings 1:8 NASB). But not even the pomp and power of a king could make Elijah back down when it came to the worship of the true God.

Elijah performed many miracles, the most spectacular coming in a show-down with four hundred prophets of Baal. Through Elijah, God reasserted his lordship over Israel. Later in his career, Elijah took on a protégé, a prophet named Elisha. The two of them worked side by side, walking all around Israel, proclaiming the Word of God.

When Elijah's work on earth was done, he and Elisha took one last walk. They were going across the Jordan, and they knew that Elijah would be going away. When they reached the river, Elijah took off his mantle, which was a kind of cloak, folded it, and struck the water. The river split like the Red Sea had split for the children of Israel in Exodus, and the two prophets walked to the other side.

After Elijah and Elisha said their good-byes, a chariot of fire and horses of fire came between them. Then a whirlwind came and carried Elijah away. It was the last anyone ever saw of him. Elisha mourned for his old mentor; he tore his clothes for grief. But then he picked up Elijah's mantle from the ground and returned to the river. "Where is the LORD, the God of Elijah?" he asked (2 Kings 2:14 NASB). Then he struck the water with the mantle, and the waters split just as they had for Elijah. The prophet's authority had passed to Elisha.

No end could have been more appropriate for the fiery prophet's life, who was himself like a whirlwind.

Henry Gariepy

Take a closer look at the whirlwind that whisked Elijah into heaven. Elijah, Elisha, and even fifty of Elijah's followers somehow knew the great prophet was going to be carried into the sky that day. When that heavenly chariot pulled up, surely the two prophets thought it was Elijah's ride. So why was he transported by a whirlwind instead?

One can only speculate, but maybe it had something to do with the kind of person Elijah had been. He was a simple man. Chariots and horses were symbols of the kind of earthly power that Elijah had made a career of speaking out against. There's something appropriate about Elijah, the rough-and-ready, hairy wild man, traveling in a dusty whirlwind instead of a glorious chariot.

Then there's the fact that the whirlwind is a force of nature. Baal was supposed to be a nature god. The centerpiece of Elijah's miraculous career was his causing it not to rain for several years, demonstrating that God, not Baal, was in charge of nature. The true God of nature could have carried his servant home in a grand, gleaming chariot. This time, however, he chose to do his work through a familiar force of nature.

> *Put your ear to the earth—learn the basics. Listen—the fish in the ocean will tell you their stories. Isn't it clear that they all know and agree that GOD is sovereign, that he holds all things in his hand?*
>
> Job 12:8–9 MSG

Which is more miraculous, a fiery chariot from heaven, or a whirlwind? When it comes to "wow" factor, even a whirlwind strong enough to pick up a man and carry him away was pretty bland next to a fiery chariot drawn by fiery horses.

Apply It
to Your Life

One thing Elijah's experience teaches is that a miracle doesn't have to be flashy to be a miracle. People tend to define a miracle as something that goes against the laws of nature. But isn't nature itself a miracle? The God of nature created everything there is out of pure nothingness. That means everything you see is a miracle, the work of God.

Sure, there's nothing flashy about the "coincidences" that have shaped your life—the person you met only once who gave you a new way of thinking about things, the phone call you missed that would have gotten you in big trouble, the very fact that your parents met and had you instead of meeting somebody else and having other kids. But all those occurrences add up to a miraculous life. Maybe you'll experience something as awe-inspiring as a fiery chariot someday. But for now, you might want to look for the miraculous in your everyday life.

I don't believe in miracles. I depend upon them.
Raymond Dale

In *The World According to Narnia,* Jonathan Rogers talks about the idea of finding the miraculous in everyday life:

"The created world is fraught with magic. Behind the most mundane of earthly beings, objects, and events is a meaning and power no less awe-inspiring than the Word of God that spoke the whole thing into existence. Yes, this is a fallen world. Dangers and temptations lurk everywhere. And yet the created order is also the raw material for a life of virtue."

Elijah's miracles demonstrated that God, not Baal, is the true God of nature. C. S. Lewis makes the same point in *Miracles*:

"It is He who sends rain into the furrows till the valleys stand so thick with corn that they laugh and sing. The trees of the wood rejoice before Him . . . He is the God of wheat and oil. In that respect He is constantly doing all the things that Nature-Gods do: He is Bacchus, Venus, Ceres all rolled into one."

Zooming In

You may have heard the phrase "take up the mantle." When the CEO of a company retires, for instance, his successor is sometimes said to "take up his mantle." That phrase comes from Elisha taking up Elijah's mantle at the river Jordan. In that act, he became the true successor to his mentor.

Because Elijah went to heaven without dying, later generations of Jews came to believe that he would come back to earth to live out the rest of his life. Some even believed the Messiah would be the returning Elijah. That's why John the Baptist's followers asked him if he was Elijah.

Through the
Eyes of
Your Heart

Think about some times you've experienced amazing "coincidences." What do those experiences tell you about the way God works?

_____

_____

_____

_____

Spend some time looking at a leaf—really looking at it, for longer than you've ever looked at a leaf before. What does that leaf tell you about the way God works?

_____

_____

_____

Consider the best relationships in your life and the worst. What do those relationships tell you about the way God works?

_____

_____

_____

_____

God in the Dark Places

From my youth,
I have been afflicted and near death.
I suffer Your horrors; I am desperate.
Your wrath sweeps over me;
Your terrors destroy me.
They surround me like water all day long;
they close in on me from every side.
You have distanced loved one and neighbor from me;
darkness is my [only] friend.

Psalm 88:15–18 HCSB

The Big Picture

One of the incredible things about the book of Psalms is its human honesty. David and the other psalmists pour their hearts out in these poems; all their joy, all their anger, all their confusion, everything they experience is right there on the page for all the world to see. And sometimes, as you can read for yourself, the psalmists feel things they aren't supposed to feel. You're not supposed to be angry at God, are you? And yet there are several places in the Psalms where the poet expresses real frustration, not with life in general, but with God himself. If you take these psalms out of context, you could really get the wrong idea about what the Bible teaches.

In almost every case, however, the writer works through his issues over the course of the psalm. He may start out angry, frustrated, even rebellious, but by the end of the psalm, he is ready to surrender again, to worship God.

These psalms offer up beautiful examples of people struggling through hardship and coming out on the other side with even greater faith.

The exception to that rule is Psalm 88. This one doesn't have a happy ending. It begins with a complaint: the psalmist has prayed to be delivered from trouble, but no deliverance has come. "I have had enough troubles," he says (v. 3 HCSB). He has lost his strength. He has been put into a pit. He has lost his friends. He doesn't mind blaming God, either. "*You* have overwhelmed me," he prays (v. 7 HCSB). "*You* have made me repulsive" (v. 8 HCSB, italics added).

Verse 13 seems to offer some hope. This is where these psalms of complaint usually turn around. "But I call to you for help, Lord." *Now*, you think, *now this poor guy's finally going to get some relief.* He's calling out to God, and God will surely answer. But the psalmist doesn't get any relief. That final third of the psalm, usually so positive even in the psalms of complaint, is just as dark as the first two-thirds, maybe worse. "LORD, why do You reject me? . . . Your terrors destroy me" (vv. 14, 16 HCSB). When Psalm 88 ends, the psalmist is still walking in sorrow. And the reader is left to wonder, what on earth is going on here?

The riddles of God are more satisfying than the solutions of man.

G. K. Chesterton

Maybe the way to make sense of Psalm 88 is not only to take a closer look at it, but also to take a step back and look at all the other psalms of complaint. It would be a mistake to take this one psalm as the standard for how believers ought to think about God. The despair in this psalm is more than overbalanced by the hope in the rest of the psalms, even those that start out as bitter complaints. Hope, not sorrow, is the message of the Bible.

So why is this psalm included in the Scriptures at all? Because this is how even true believers feel sometimes. God always delivers, but not always as quickly as you think he ought to. He might have reasons for leaving you in a difficult situation—reasons the human mind won't understand this side of heaven. And when you're in trouble, and you feel God isn't listening, despair can creep in. That's why there is a strange comfort in this very uncomfortable psalm. You feel guilty for doubting God, even for being mad at God. Psalm 88 makes you realize that even people as godly as the psalmists have that experience from time to time.

For just as the heavens are higher than the earth, so are my ways higher than your ways and my thoughts higher than your thoughts.

Isaiah 55:9 NLT

You're at a time in your life when a lot of things just don't make sense. Everything changes so fast, both inside and outside of you. Sometimes you feel angry or depressed or frustrated, and you don't even understand why. That's hard enough to deal with without church people telling you you're supposed to be hap-hap-happy all the time-

**Apply It
to Your Life**

time-time. Life isn't church camp. God never intended for you to live on an emotional mountaintop all the time. Troubles and hardship are an important part of growing up, and you don't have to grin and bear it all the time; nor do you have to pretend everything's okay. Get mad. Get frustrated. Ask God why. He can handle it. If you deal honestly with your emotions, you're going to learn how to experience an inner life that's pleasing to God.

Psalm 88 is a great place to go when you feel God isn't listening. Let yourself be reminded that being frustrated with God doesn't mean you've totally lost your faith. But don't stop at Psalm 88. Read the other psalms to see how other godly people worked through their anger and were again able to say, "Blessed be the Lord forever" (Psalm 89:52 NASB).

God does not make our lives all shipshape, clear and comfortable. . . . In this mixed-up life there is always an element of unclearness. I believe God wills it so.

Baron Friedrich von Hügel

D. A. Carson notes that the most important thing to remember about Psalm 88 is the fact that even though the psalmist is going through a struggle, he's still serious about seeking God:

"The cries and hurts penned here are not the cheap and thoughtless rage of people who use their darker moments to denounce God from afar, the smug critique of supercilious agnosticism or arrogant atheism. These cries actively engage with God, fully aware of the only real source of help."

Mike Mason, writing in *The Gospel According to Job*, finds hope in Psalm 88:

"The true believer does not always rise from his knees full of encouragement and fresh hope. There are times when one may remain down in the dumps and yet still have prayed well. For what God wants from us is not the observance of religious protocol, but just that we be real with Him. What He wants is our heart."

Zooming **In**

Psalm 88 is not one of David's psalms, but a "psalm of the sons of Korah." The descendants of Korah were a clan within the priestly tribe of Levi. The Korahites specialized in various jobs related to temple worship. Some were temple gate-keepers, some baked showbread (unleavened loaves of bread for the altar), and some were temple singers.

At least a third of the 150 psalms can be considered psalms of lament—psalms that deal with human trouble and the struggle to keep the faith in spite of it. All of these psalms—with the exception of Psalm 88—move from the darkness of suffering into the light of God's deliverance.

Even the strongest believers go through rough patches when they experience doubts—even doubts about God's very existence. The important thing is to be honest with God and with yourself. God does some of his best, most lasting work in those times when it's hard to see he's there.

Through the
Eyes of
Your Heart

What is the difference between honest doubts and losing your faith?

_____

_____

_____

_____

What is it that causes you to have doubts about God's goodness or even God's existence?

_____

_____

_____

Write out a prayer in which you are perfectly honest with God about how you feel about things. You don't have to dress it up with pretty language or overly spiritual thoughts. God knows your heart already; he just wants you to be honest.

_____

_____

_____

_____

Light for the Path

Your word is a lamp to my feet and a light to my path.
I have sworn an oath and confirmed it, to keep your
righteous rules.

Psalm 119:105–106 ESV

The Big Picture

Clocking in at a whopping 176 verses, Psalm 119 is the longest chapter in all of Scripture. The second-longest chapter in the Bible (Numbers 7) is barely half as long. Psalm 119 is different from most of the other psalms; instead of reading like a single poem tightly organized around a central thought or theme, this psalm is a big, sprawling, almost stream-of-consciousness collection of ideas exploring every nook and cranny of a very broad theme: the psalmist's love of the Word of God. "How can a young man keep his way pure? By keeping it according to Your word" (verse 9 NASB). "Forever, O LORD, Your word is settled in heaven" (verse 89 NASB). "O how I love Your law!" (verse 97 NASB). "Rescue me, for I do not forget Your law" (verse 153 NASB).

The commentator Matthew Henry speculated that Psalm 119 may have been a collection of David's short prayers and thoughts that he wrote down in his journal over the years. That's just one man's guess, of course, but it would help explain why the ideas in this psalm are so wide-ranging and

take a **CLOSER** look for teens

seemingly disconnected, why they sometimes seem redundant. Psalm 119 isn't so much a chain of gold links, said Matthew Henry, as a treasure chest full of golden rings. In other words, each part is beautifully and skillfully wrought, but the parts don't necessarily hang together as a nice, organized whole.

One of the most well-known of this psalm's 176 verses is verse 105: "Your word is a lamp to my feet and a light to my path." This one verse, as much as any one verse can, captures the spirit of this great and diverse psalm. In the midst of a dark and confusing world, God's Word provides guidance. It is a light in the darkness, and a lamp to guide your steps when things just don't make sense. You don't have to have everything figured out; God's Word lights the way, step-by-step, whatever turns your path might take. This verse has always been a source of comfort and hope to God's people. Almost in the very middle of the Bible, this great psalm is like the massive cornerstone of Scripture, assuring the people of God that they really can base their whole lives on God's Word.

The Bible is meant not only to inform,
but to transform.

Author unknown

It's one of the most well-known verses in all of Scripture: "Your word is a lamp to my feet and a light to my path." But how many people know the next verse? "I have sworn an oath and confirmed it, to keep your righteous rules." Why was the psalmist so confident in God's guidance? Because he had committed to conforming himself to God's law. He submitted to God's ways. He promised to stay on God's path. And so he reaped the reward: a well-lit path where he could safely walk with confidence.

Throughout Psalm 119, the psalmist speaks not only about the greatness of God's Word, but also his own commitment to follow it. The perfection of the law isn't just something to marvel at, but something to respond to. And, in one of those great paradoxes that appear throughout the Bible, submitting to God's law turns out to be the only way to enjoy freedom. "I will walk at liberty, for I seek Your precepts" (verse 45 NASB). The law of God doesn't save you. But it can save you a whole lot of heartache if you, like the psalmist, commit to keep God's "righteous rules."

> All flesh is like grass and all its glory like the flower of grass. The grass withers, and the flower falls, but the word of the Lord endures forever.
>
> 1 Peter 1:24–25 NRSV

It's a source of great comfort and hope to know that even in the hard times, the Word of God lights your way. But don't forget the rest of the story: if you want to enjoy the benefits of a lit path, you've got to commit to stay on the path. When you wander out into the woods, how can you expect to benefit from the streetlight? God's guidance isn't something to call on only when you get yourself into a mess you can't get yourself out of. If you are committed to reading God's Word every day and living out the truths you find there, you can be confident that you'll have light enough to steer around any obstacle, and guidance at every crossroads.

Apply It to Your Life

Of course God can rescue those who get off the path; he does it all the time. He can untangle you from the underbrush and set you back on the straight and narrow. But how much better never to leave the path at all? There's real joy, real freedom in walking in God's ways. If you are committed to keeping God's "righteous rules," your daily Bible reading will be a matter of course-correction, not emergency roadside assistance.

The Bible is the greatest benefit which the human race has ever experienced. A single line in the Bible has consoled me more than all the books I ever read besides.

Immanuel Kant

John Wesley wore himself to a frazzle trying to get to heaven in his own efforts. At last he surrendered to God's way. He had a whole new outlook on life, and on the Bible:

"I want to know one thing, the way to heaven: how to land safe on that happy shore. God himself has condescended to teach the way; for this very end he came from heaven. He has written it down in a book! Oh, give me that book! At any price, give me the book of God!"

The novelist known as George Eliot (actually a woman named Mary Ann Evans) offers this insight into the relationship between our obedience and God's guidance:

"As soon as we lay ourselves entirely at His feet, we have enough light given to us to guide our own steps. We are like the foot soldier, who hears nothing of the councils that determine the course of the great battle he is in, but hears plainly enough the word of command that he must himself obey."

Zooming **In**

Psalm 119 is an acrostic poem. It's divided into eight-verse stanzas, one for each of the twenty-two letters of the Hebrew alphabet. In the original Hebrew, each verse in each stanza began with the same letter. In the first stanza, each verse begins with the letter *aleph*, the first letter of the alphabet. In the second stanza, each begins with *beth*, all the way through to the twenty-second stanza, which begins with *tav*, the twenty-second and final letter. So even if the ideas in this psalm seem sprawling and even a little unorganized at first glance, its structure shows that it is actually a very well-thought-out piece of poetry.

Through the **Eyes of** Your Heart

Where else do people look for illumination besides God's Word? Do you find yourself looking to those places, too?

_____

_____

_____

_____

Psalm 119 speaks of the freedom that comes from submitting yourself to the laws of God. What do you think that means?

_____

_____

_____

_____

Can you say, like the psalmist, "O how I love Your law"? Why or why not?

_____

_____

_____

_____

Be Reasonable!

Come now, let us reason together, says the LORD:
though your sins are like scarlet,
they shall be as white as snow;
though they are red like crimson,
they shall become like wool.
Isaiah 1:18 ESV

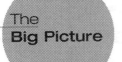

The Big Picture

You may think the word *prophecy* means the same thing as *prediction*. The Old Testament prophets definitely made some amazing predictions that came true, sometimes centuries later. But forecasting the future was actually a comparatively small part of their job. In the Old Testament, God sent prophets to stir things up, to speak hard truths when their society had gotten out of line with God's plans.

Perhaps Martin Luther King Jr. is a good comparison to help understand the role of the prophets in Israelite society. A man of God in a turbulent era in American history, King looked around at his society and saw that it had strayed far from God's plan. He spoke out against the injustices of segregation and racism not merely on political or legal grounds, but on biblical grounds. His vision of a better future offered hope, but it also angered a lot of people who didn't appreciate being told that they were wrong. Whether or not Martin Luther King Jr. was a prophet in a literal sense, his life at least offers a good analogy for understanding the work of a prophet like Isaiah.

The book of Isaiah begins with some very hard truths. The people of Israel had revolted against God. "An ox knows its owner, and a donkey its master's manger, but Israel does not know, My people do not understand" (1:3 NASB). God's people had grown more stupid and less reasonable than farm animals. In its corruption, the nation was overrun by enemies. Meanwhile, the Israelites were still going through the motions of religion. But in the absence of obedience and social justice, all that religious rigmarole just made God more angry. "Cease to do evil," God said. "Learn to do good; seek justice . . . defend the orphan, plead for the widow" (vv. 16–17 NASB). In other words, if the people of Israel expect God to accept their religious activities, they'd better get serious about obeying God in other areas of life.

Then, in verse 18, God's tone totally changes. "Come now, let us reason together, says the LORD: though your sins are like scarlet, they shall be as white as snow." The rising voice of God's frustration with his rebellious people gives way to a quiet promise of cleansing and forgiveness. It sounds almost as if God is reining himself in: Let's be reasonable. Let's not argue. Here's hope for a new future—if only you will take this opportunity to turn back.

The ultimate purpose of reason is to bring us to the place where we see that there is a limit to reason.

Blaise Pascal

**Take a
Closer Look**

The definition of insanity, it has been said, is doing the same things you've always done, the same way you've always done them, and expecting a different result. That's the kind of insanity that the people of Israel had fallen into. They had let their society stray far from God's plan. They were "weighed down with iniquity" (v. 4 NASB). They weren't taking care of the weakest people in their society (the widows and orphans). Ruthless people were running loose. All that corruption weakened their society and made them easy pickings for their enemies. So they prayed for relief. They gave offerings. They held festivals. They did every religious activity they could think of, trying to get God to come to their aid. But God paid no attention to all that empty religion because the rest of their lives showed that their hearts were far away from God.

The people of Israel did the same things over and over again—the same old sin and injustice, the same old empty religion—but they were hoping for a different outcome. In response to that unreasonable expectation, God says, "Come, let us reason together." Want a different outcome? Try some different input. It's only reasonable.

> *Real wisdom, God's wisdom, begins with a holy life and is characterized by getting along with others. It is gentle and reasonable.*
>
> James 3:17 MSG

It's easy to recognize when somebody else is being unreasonable. Look at the people of Isaiah's day "multiplying prayers" and going through all those religious motions while they were acting like jerks the rest of the time. Of course God didn't hear those prayers. What did they expect? It's not so easy to see that kind of irrationality in your own life. Maybe it's time to take a step back and look at yourself with the same objectivity with which you look at other people. Does your day-to-day life square up with your life on Sundays? Or do your actions Monday through Saturday suggest that your Sunday activities are just empty ritual?

When God called the Israelites to be reasonable, he gave them a choice: "If you consent and obey, you will eat the best of the land; but if you refuse and rebel, you will be devoured by the sword" (Isaiah 1:19–20 NASB). Okay, if you disobey, there probably won't be a swordsman on your doorstep tomorrow. But the principle holds: bad choices devour your life, and good choices secure God's best for your life. Are you going to make the reasonable choice?

Holy Spirit, think through me until your ideas are my ideas.
Amy Carmichael

David Littleton Baker collected short letters he had written to his son into the book *Advice to My Son D. L. from Proverbs*. Here's what he said about God's invitation, "Come let us reason together."

"The man right before God is a thoughtful man, because he serves a thoughtful God. God has given us the ability to think logically. He delights to sit down with us and reflect through the implications of what we are doing or saying. . . . He wants us to ask Him about things and He delights for us to seek them out."

Sometimes reason is presented as the opposite of faith—as if you had to reject one to have the other. Here's what Dwight A. Moody says about that:

"Reason is not the evil enemy of faith. Reason is a God-given process of the human mind. . . . With our reason we discern the truth of Scripture. . . . The Spirit of God speaks to us through our reason. . . . What we do reject is a secular, anti-spiritual, anti-supernatural bias that predisposes us to certain conclusions in the reasoning process."

Zooming **In**

When prophets in the Bible predicted the future, they were often speaking about a *conditional* future: *if* you continue to do these things, *then* you can expect this kind of future, or *if* you start doing these other things, *then* you can expect a better future. Which means that the prophets were often making predictions that they hoped would not come true. The important thing wasn't the prophets' ability to accurately discern some unavoidable future, but their call to make better choices in the present. Of course, when the Hebrew people refused to listen to the prophets, the prophets' dire predictions proved all too true.

Sometimes people think of faith and reason as being enemies of each other; faith, by their definition, is irrational. But the Bible makes it clear that faith heals the insanity, the irrationality of a life apart from God. Faith re-centers you, restores your perspective, resets your equilibrium.

Through the
Eyes of
Your Heart

Is there some part of your life that has gotten out of balance, out of perspective? How can the truths of Scripture restore sanity?

_____

_____

_____

How closely does your Monday-through-Saturday life square with your life on Sunday? What adjustments might you need to make to get back in balance?

_____

_____

_____

Where do you think people get the idea that following God's path means throwing reason out the window?

_____

_____

_____

The Prophet Who Was All Wet

Jonah answered, "I'm a Hebrew, and I worship the LORD God of heaven, who made the sea and the dry land." When the sailors heard this, they were frightened, because Jonah had already told them he was running from the LORD. Then they said, "Do you know what you have done?"

Jonah 1:9–10 CEV

The **Big Picture**

The wind came howling across the water, whipping the Mediterranean into huge swells that threatened to break the ship into matchsticks. The sailors threw the cargo overboard to lighten the ship—better to lose the cargo than their lives. But it didn't help. They called on their many gods. But that didn't help, either. Then the captain remembered one of the passengers, a strange fellow named Jonah, who acted like a man who had something to hide. Maybe Jonah's God could help.

The captain found the stranger below decks, sleeping in the hold. Sleeping! At a time like this! "How can you sleep at a time like this?" the captain shouted over the roar of the sea. "Get up and pray to your God! Maybe he will have pity on us and keep us from drowning" (1:6 CEV).

The sailors were superstitious, and they suspected somebody on that ship was to blame. They decided to cast lots to find out who was the jinx who had brought his bad fortune on them. Imagine how Jonah must have felt as the sailors began to cast lots. He must have known that if anyone on that ship was to blame, it was he; he, after all, was the one who was actively disobeying God by sailing to Tarshish, the other end of the world from Nineveh, the place where God had told him to go. Should he confess? But on the other hand, sometimes a storm was just a storm, right? Maybe it wasn't anybody's fault.

All eyes were on Jonah when the lot fell to him. He knew he was busted. "I'm a Hebrew," he blurted out, "and I worship the LORD God of heaven, who made the sea and the dry land." The sailors freaked. They had heard of the Hebrews' God, and they knew that he truly was the ruler of the sea, the land, and everything else. Jonah had put them in a terrible position. He had brought this storm on him, so they were afraid to keep him on board. But they were also afraid to lay a hand on a servant of the Hebrews' God. In the end, they realized that they had no choice but to throw him over. But that was part of God's plan, too. The waves grew calm, and soon thereafter a great fish came along—Jonah's alternative transportation to Nineveh.

Preach the gospel every day;
if necessary, use words.

Francis of Assisi

Take a closer look at the sailors' reaction to Jonah's announcement that he was a Hebrew. They were terrified. "How could you do this?" they gasped. In his selfishness and disobedience, Jonah didn't just bring trouble on himself. Everybody around him was affected. Because of Jonah, their lives were in peril. Because of Jonah, they lost all their cargo. You might expect them to be happy to see this troublemaker drowned. But even when Jonah told them to throw him overboard, the sailors did everything in their power to avoid it. After all that Jonah put them through, they offered up prayers as they threw him over, and they made a sacrifice to God.

The irony was that God had chosen Jonah to be the vehicle of a special blessing to those who didn't know God. When God commanded Jonah to preach to the people of Nineveh, he was reaching out to some of the most wicked, godless people on the face of the earth. Jonah ran away because he didn't *want* to see the cruel Ninevites saved. That was bad enough; but in the process, he hurt people with whom he had no quarrel.

> *You are the light of the world. A city that is set on a hill cannot be hidden.*
>
> Matthew 5:14 NKJV

It's nothing you haven't heard before: bad choices have negative results. But how much do you think about the ways your choices affect other people besides yourself? If you choose to go to a party where you know you have no business, who is affected by that? Okay, there's the possibility that you could get busted, but forget about that for a minute. What about the other person who has been thinking about straightening up but sees you there and figures it must not be so bad after all? Maybe there's a person who has been thinking about becoming a Christian but hears that you were at that party (people do love to talk, after all) and says, "Never mind—Christians are all hypocrites anyway."

If you are a believer, you are part of God's plan to bless all the nations of the earth. Obedience isn't just about your individual relationship with God. As people live the kind of lives that please God, other people reap the benefits. The world is literally a better place. Without God, people are in a sinking ship. Are you helping people get to safety, or are you making it even harder to stay afloat?

Christianity is not just Christ in you,
but Christ living his life through you.

Author unknown

How Others See It

Joni Eareckson Tada finds significance in the idea that the word *Christian* actually means "little Christ." You might say it's the first step in your Christian witness:

"What an honor to share Christ's name! We can be bold to call ourselves Christians and bear the stamp of his character and reputation. When people find out that you are a Christian, they should already have an idea of who you are and what you are simply because you bear such a precious name."

In *No More Excuses,* Tony Evans talks about the moment when the captain of Jonah's ship finds him sleeping instead of praying during the storm:

"You can get so content in rebellion that you don't even know God is after you. So here a sinner has to ask a saint, 'How come you are sleeping? You ought to be praying.' This shows how bad God's people can get. We can go so far away from God that we sleep when He is trying to deal with us."

Zooming **In**

The city of Nineveh, where God commanded Jonah to go preach, was the capital of Assyria, a powerful and unusually cruel empire. Jonah, no doubt, feared for his personal safety when God told him to go to Nineveh. But as Jonah later admitted, the big reason he ran away was that he wanted to see the Ninevites punished, not forgiven. His people had suffered much at the hands of the Assyrians, and Jonah wanted to see them get what they had coming to them. He was actually angry when the Ninevites listened to his sermon and turned to God! Some people never learn.

Spend some time thinking about consequences. For better or for worse, people are connected in an intricate web of cause and effect. Nobody is an island. That means if you choose to disobey, your actions affect others negatively. But on the flip side, when you obey, your life blesses other people.

Write about a time in your life when your disobedience had consequences for people who had done nothing wrong. Now consider the other side of the equation: when have your good choices benefited people who had nothing to do with your good choice?

_____

_____

_____

One person disobeys, and other people suffer for it. Doesn't quite seem fair. Why do you think God lets the world work that way?

_____

_____

_____

_____

The Bible makes it clear that God's people are to be a blessing to all the world. What do you think that means?

_____

_____

_____

Son of David, Son of God

> *[Jesus said,] "How is it that the scribes say that the Christ is the son of David? . . . David himself calls Him 'Lord'; so in what sense is He his son?" And the large crowd enjoyed listening to Him.*
>
> Mark 12:35, 37 NASB

The
Big Picture

Right there in the temple, on the home court of the religious experts, Jesus asked a question that challenged one of the most dearly held beliefs of the Jewish people: Why do you keep calling the Messiah the Son of David? The scribes and Pharisees must have scratched their heads. They spoke of the Messiah as the Son of David because they had always spoken of him as the Son of David. The tradition had been passed down for generations. Besides, they could point to verses in the Psalms that suggested the Messiah would be a descendant of David. What kind of question was this Jesus asking, anyway?

The Messiah, of course, *was* a descendant of David. But Jesus was asking something much bigger than a mere genealogical question. In essence, he was asking, "What makes you think the Messiah is going to be an earthly king?" The reign of King David was a high point in Jewish history. The kingdom was strong, united, and prosperous. In the centuries since that time, the Jews had been subjected to one humiliation after another. Their armies were defeated numerous times, their land was invaded by ruthless enemies, they were carried off into captivity, they went through periods of incredible idolatry and lawlessness, and now they were being ruled by the Romans in their own land. No wonder the Jews dreamed of a Messiah who would wipe out their oppressors and make them a great nation once again. They wanted a new David.

By asking the question that he asked—and by answering it—Jesus was saying, "It's time to find a new way of thinking about the Messiah. The kingdom of God is coming, but it's not going to look like you expect it to look. The Messiah may technically be a son of David, but much more important, he is the Son of God. He won't establish his kingdom by way of horses or chariots or gleaming spears. He'll establish it by way of love and hope."

And next to that kind of kingdom, a kingdom of gold crowns and scepters and palaces and armies looks puny indeed. Even David himself bowed low before the true Messiah. No, the Messiah wasn't the Son of David, even if that's what his lineage suggested. He was the Son of God.

The only significance of life consists in helping
to establish the kingdom of God.

Leo Tolstoy

Check out the crowd's reaction in this passage: "the large crowd enjoyed listening to Him." No doubt the crowd took some pleasure in seeing a simple carpenter's son standing up to the know-it-all scribes, the gatekeepers of all religious experience for the Jews. The scribes expected the Messiah to deliver them from political oppression. The irony was that the scribes were themselves oppressors. Jesus said they "devour widows' houses, and for apearance's sake offer long prayers" (Mark 12:40 NASB). The scribes had no idea that hypocrisy of that kind was one of the first things the Messiah would deal with. He would do his work from the inside out, changing *people,* not regimes.

The crowd could sense that, and they appreciated it. The Jewish people hated living under the oppression of the Romans. But they also lived under the oppression of religious professionals who added rules and obligations to the law of God in order to maintain their power. Jesus came to deliver people from that kind of oppression first. At this moment the crowd seemed to understand that in spite of what they had always thought, their first need wasn't political deliverance. They needed the kingdom of God, not another kingdom of David.

> *Seek first the kingdom of God and His righteousness, and all these things shall be added to you.*
>
> Matthew 6:33 NKJV

Sometimes you look at your life and think all you need is a change of circumstances. You'd be happy if only the school's social hierarchy were overturned and you had a fair shot at being popular. You'd be content if only you had a little more spending money or a decent car. You'd never ask God for another thing if only your home life weren't so messed up and your parents would just get a clue.

But the kingdom of God isn't about changing your circumstances—at least that's not primarily what it's about. The kingdom of God is about changing you first. Sure, your outward circumstances may improve as you get your life in order. But whether they do or don't improve, the important thing is knowing that your citizenship isn't here on earth anyway.

The Jews of Jesus' day thought the Messiah was going to come to them as the new David, setting their earthly kingdom to rights. But when Jesus left the earth, the Romans were still running things. That didn't change. What changed was the fact that Jesus made a new way for people to relate to God and to one another. The Son of God changed the world from the inside out.

There can be no kingdom of God in the world without the kingdom of God in our hearts.

Albert Schweitzer

From his *Commentary on the Gospel According to Matthew*, Floyd Filson remarked on what it meant for Jesus to downplay the idea that the Messiah was the Son of David:

"At the very least Jesus declares the freedom of the Messiah to establish the Kingdom by another path than the political and military methods of David. The Messiah can be and will be the Suffering Servant rather than the military conqueror and earthly king."

In *The Secret Message of Jesus,* Brian McLaren discusses what Jesus meant by "the kingdom of God." He wasn't talking about "heaven after you die," but something here and now:

"Maybe the meaning would be clearer if we paraphrased it like this: 'You're all preoccupied with the oppressive empire of Caesar and the oppressed kingdom of Israel. You're missing the point: the kingdom of God is here now, available to all! This is the reality that matters most. Believe the good news and follow me!'"

Zooming **In**

The fact that Jesus was a "son of David" accounts for his being born in Bethlehem instead of Nazareth, where his parents lived. The Romans required everyone to go to his family's place of origin to register. Joseph, being a descendant of David, traveled with Mary to Bethlehem, the town of David.

In the time of Jesus, the group of Jews that was most eager to greet a conquering Messiah was known as the Zealots. They were convinced that the way of the Messiah was one of physical violence against the Jews' oppressors, the Romans. They frequently fought the Romans—not head-on, but in small-scale guerrilla or terrorist actions.

> *When Jesus spoke of the kingdom of God, he wasn't suggesting that the kingdoms of earth should never change or that God was only concerned with spiritual things. But he was saying that the only earthly changes that count or that can last are those that begin with people who are changed on the inside.*

Through the
Eyes of
Your Heart

Why was Jesus so insistent that the Messiah wasn't going to be a new David? Didn't he want to see his people delivered from oppression?

_____

_____

_____

_____

As a Christian, what should you think of charities and social programs that seek to improve people's outward circumstances? In what ways do those programs obey the command of Jesus to love your neighbor? What are the limitations of those programs?

_____

_____

_____

Do you know people whose inward change has resulted in changes for the better in the "real world"? What do those people have in common?

_____

_____

_____

"Do You Want to Get Well?"

When Jesus saw him stretched out by the pool and knew how long he had been there, he said, "Do you want to get well?" The sick man said, "Sir, when the water is stirred, I don't have anybody to put me in the pool. By the time I get there, somebody else is already in."

Jesus said, "Get up, take your bedroll, start walking."

John 5:6–8 MSG

The
Big Picture

He had been sick for thirty-eight years. The Bible doesn't specify what exactly was wrong with the man—paralysis of some kind, presumably. In any case, he wasn't able to move very well under his own power. Thirty-eight years! No healing, no real hope. He spent his days beside the pool at Bethesda, hoping for a miracle. It was supposed to be a healing pool. Every now and then its waters bubbled—touched by an angel, people said. And according to tradition, the first person to get into the pool after it started bubbling would be healed of whatever ailment he or she suffered from.

You can imagine what a scene that was. In a world without neurosurgery or physical therapy or even wheelchairs or guide dogs, the lame and blind and chronically ill must have flocked to the pool at Bethesda. They had nowhere else to turn. And when the waters began to bubble, there must have been a mad scramble as desperate people pushed and elbowed to be the person to benefit from the healing power. Which brings us back to the sick man we began with. If you can't walk and you've got nobody to carry you, how are you supposed to be the first guy in the pool? Day in and day out, the man lay beside the healing waters, but he had no real hope of being healed. Try to imagine the frustration, the bitterness that he felt as he spent his life watching other people, not quite as sick as he was, stepping over him to get to the water he so desperately needed.

One day Jesus came to the pool and saw the man lying there. "Do you want to get well?" he asked. You can hear the man's defeated spirit in his answer: "I don't have anybody to put me in the pool. By the time I get there, somebody else is already in." But Jesus didn't need a bubbling pool or an angel's finger to heal a person. He only had to say the word. "Get up," he said. "Take your bedroll, start walking." And so the man did. His days at the healing pool resulted in healing after all—though not in the way he expected.

Joy runs deeper than despair.
Helen Keller

Take a closer look at the sick man's answer to Jesus' question. It was a simple, yes-no question: "Do you want to get well?" But the man didn't answer it. He rushed ahead with his list of frustrations and grievances he had been stewing over for years. "You don't understand . . . I'm in an impossible situation here. . . ." You can't exactly blame the guy. The world had been pretty cruel to him. The whole system seemed to be against him: those who were in most desperate need of healing were the least likely to get to the healing waters. And in all the time he had been going to the pool, nobody had ever said, "Here, you go first." Nor had anybody who beat him to the punch ever come back and said, "Now that I've been healed, let me stick around and help you next time the waters bubble."

But Jesus spoke into a life full of defeat and said, in effect, "Forget about the system. Forget about the insensitivity of all those other people; those people feel desperate, too, you know. I'm here. I'm the healer. That pool's got nothing on me. Pick up your bedroll and start walking."

> And a leper came to [Jesus] and bowed down before Him, and said, "Lord, if You are willing, You can make me clean." Jesus stretched out His hand and touched him, saying, "I am willing; be cleansed." And immediately his leprosy was cleansed.
>
> Matthew 8:2–3 NASB

The world promises wholeness and happiness. But, like the paralytic beside the pool at Bethesda, you find that the world's promise is always just out of reach. You can't quite get there. Somebody always beats you to the punch. Somebody else wins the prize. You finally make the varsity team, only to learn that it's not enough to make the

team; now you want to be all-region. Or, what's worse, maybe you *do* make all-region, or all-state, or valedictorian, and you realize that none of those things can fulfill the need you have inside. We're all broken in ways that the things of earth can't fix.

In the midst of disappointment, Jesus says, "Do you want to get well?" The temptation is to rush ahead without really answering the question. "You wouldn't believe how tough it is out there. There's an in-crowd and then there's everybody else, and if you're not in the in-crowd. . . . And my family is nuts; how can I ever expect to be normal with that bunch? . . . And I've got all these fears and doubts. . . ." But it's a simple, yes-no question: Do you want to get well? If the answer is yes, Jesus can make you well, in spite of all that junk.

We follow a gospel which says that when I am weak, then I am strong. And this gospel is the only thing that brings healing.

N. T. Wright

R. Kent Hughes reflects on Jesus' seemingly obvious question to the paralytic: "Do you want to get well?" It's not as obvious as it would seem.

"That is the great question we must face. If you are not a believer, I am responsible to pass on to you Christ's question: Do you want to get well? Do you really want to be healed? Do you truly want to be forgiven and made new? Because if you want to, you can be healed right now. If you remain unconverted even though you have a knowledge of Christ in your life, it is because you choose to be lame."

What were Jesus' healings and other miracles all about? Here's what Brian McLaren has to say about that:

"They are dramatic enactments of his message; they are the message of the kingdom spread in media beyond words. They combine to signify that the impossible is about to become possible: the kingdom of God—with its peace, healing, sanity, empowerment, and freedom—is available to all, here and now."

Zooming In

Check out this story in the New International version of the Bible (NIV). It's John 5:1–9. Notice anything strange about the verse numbers? There's no verse 4. Some early manuscripts don't include the part about the angel stirring the waters of the pool, so the translators of the NIV chose to leave that verse out.

Archaeologists believe that they have identified the location of the Pool of Bethesda. It is near the eastern wall of Jerusalem, close to St. Stephen's Gate. It is actually two pools with a walkway between them. Archaeologists have found the five porticoes around the pools, just as the Bible describes.

*Jesus offers healing. Your problems may be caused by
a whole complicated web of earthly causes and effects,
but that doesn't mean the solutions to your problems
lie in earthly causes and effects. God cuts right through
all that to offer healing—healing that comes first to
your heart and mind.*

What is the litany of challenges and difficulties that limit your life and keep
you from being everything God wants you to be? Write out the list.

_____

_____

_____

How can God overcome all those things?

_____

_____

_____

Do you want to be healed? (One-word answers only, please.)

_____

_____

_____

The Woman Who Reached Out

And behold, a woman . . . came up behind him and touched the fringe of his garment, for she said to herself, "If I only touch his garment, I will be made well." Jesus turned, and seeing her he said, "Take heart, daughter; your faith has made you well." And instantly the woman was made well.

Matthew 9:20–22 ESV

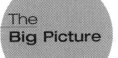

The Big Picture

Nobody ever seemed to be neutral about Jesus. Some people loved him. Some people hated him. Many people changed their minds about him, going from one extreme to another. In the land of the Gerasenes, the people demanded that he go away after he healed a demon-possessed man and cast the demons into a herd of pigs. Nobody, after all, wants demon-possessed pigs (not to mention the fact that the pigs all jumped off a cliff and drowned—not good for the guy who owned the pigs). So Jesus got in a boat and crossed the water to the area called Decapolis.

The Gerasenes couldn't wait to see Jesus go, but here on the other side of the water, the people couldn't wait for his boat to land. A crowd gathered by the shore, desperate for the touch of the Healer. Among that crowd was a synagogue official named Jairus. He was an important man, yet he fell at Jesus' feet and begged him to come heal his daughter who was at the point of death. Jesus followed the man toward the house where the little girl lay, and the crowd came along, bumping and jostling.

Somewhere in that crowd was another sufferer, not nearly as important a person—on the social ladder—as Jairus. She had been suffering from a hemorrhage of some sort for twelve years. She had been to every doctor she could find; they had subjected her to all sorts of treatments, and the doctors had taken all her money. But nothing helped. The woman managed to push through the crowd to get to Jesus. She was convinced that if she could only get one finger on the edge of Jesus' garment, she would be healed. She was right. The instant she touched him, she could tell that the internal bleeding was cured after twelve years.

Jesus stopped in his tracks. Imagine what Jairus must have been thinking: "Don't stop! We don't have a minute to waste! My daughter is dying!" But Jesus stopped when he felt the power go out of him. "Who touched me?" he asked. (See the same story in Luke 8:42–48.) His disciples thought he must have been joking. A hundred people had touched Jesus in that bumping, jostling crowd. But the woman knew what Jesus was talking about. Terrified, she fell at Jesus' feet and tried to explain her boldness. Jesus' look of tenderness dispelled her fear. "Daughter," he said, "your faith has made you well."

God heals, and the doctor takes the fee.
Benjamin Franklin

The boldness of the woman in this story deserves a closer look. It was no easy thing for her to push through the crowd to touch Jesus, and not just because her illness probably left her physically weak. There were a number of social pressures that might have held her back. She was poor. She was sick. She was a woman in a society that didn't think very highly of women. In short, she was very, very low in the pecking order of that society. And Jesus had already committed to helping Jairus, who, being a religious official, was quite high in the pecking order. But the woman wouldn't be denied. She touched the hem of Jesus' robe, and everything stopped.

The woman's terrified reaction when Jesus turned around—recorded in Luke 8—gives you some idea of what a risk she was taking. "Then the woman, seeing that she could not go unnoticed, came trembling and fell at his feet. In the presence of all the people, she told why she had touched him and how she had been instantly healed" (Luke 8:47 NIV). How dare a lowly creature like her touch the great Teacher? What might Jairus do to her for delaying the healing of his daughter? But Jesus cared nothing for social rank. In the woman's act of desperation and hope, he saw the raw materials for a miracle. God himself stopped everything to serve a woman when no one else would.

> *Draw near to God, and he will draw near to you.*
>
> James 4:8 NRSV

God invites you to come boldly before his throne and make your requests known to him, just as the woman with the hemorrhage did. It's a tricky balance between humility and boldness—confidence that God welcomes you into his presence and an understanding of your own need. You may not feel very important. But when you reach out to God, he responds immediately.

Apply It to Your Life

The woman took major risks and went to major trouble in order to touch the hem of Jesus' garment. Why? Because she realized she had nowhere else to turn. She had tried everything else in the world, and none of it helped. Everybody else had left her in as bad a condition as they found her. Sound desperate? Maybe a better word is *radical*. The woman's gamble paid off in a big way.

When you realize you've got nothing to lose, you're a prime candidate for a miracle. Push through the crowd. Reach out to Jesus. He won't leave you hanging; he'll come through every time.

There is a light in this world, a healing spirit more powerful than any darkness we may encounter.

Mother Teresa

In his *Gospel According to Mark,* James R. Edwards points out that for the synagogue official Jairus, the sick woman wasn't just an interruption, but an example:

"When Jesus says, 'Don't be afraid; just believe,' how should Jairus understand the command to believe? What kind of faith should he have? The answer is that he must have the kind of faith the woman has! The woman exemplifies and defines faith for Jairus, which means to trust Jesus despite everything to the contrary. That faith knows no limits—not even the raising of a dead child!"

J. Dwight Pentecost sees great meaning in the woman's gesture of kneeling to touch the hem of Jesus' robe:

"The woman's action was significant. A subject knelt to touch the hem of a king's robe to show loyalty and submission to his authority. Such an action preceded the presentation of a request to the king by the subject. Hence the woman's act showed here recognition of the royal authority that belonged to Christ. This was the basis of her request for help. This was the touch of faith, and it is recorded that 'immediately her bleeding stopped.'"

Zooming **In**

The woman's hemorrhage in this story probably was related to her menstrual cycle, which would mean that on top of all her other problems, she had been ceremonially unclean for twelve years. She would have been forbidden from entering places of worship or from sitting down at the table with other people. The very fact that she was out in a crowd of people would have been a violation of Jewish practice, for an "unclean" person was in danger of contaminating everybody he or she came into contact with. You can imagine what an isolating—not to mention embarrassing—condition hers would have been.

The Bible promises that if you draw near to God, God will draw near to you. All you have to do is to reach out your hand, just as the woman in Decapolis reached out to Jesus. She wasn't disappointed.

What, if anything, holds you back from reaching out to Jesus?

_____

_____

_____

_____

How does boldness before God relate to humility before God? How do these two seemingly contradictory things coexist?

_____

_____

_____

_____

Do you relate more to Jairus or to the woman in this story? In spite of all their differences, how were these two people alike?

_____

_____

_____

_____

From Sickbed to Service

> *When Jesus went into Peter's house, He saw his mother-in-law lying in bed with a fever. So He touched her hand, and the fever left her. Then she got up and began to serve Him.*
>
> Matthew 8:14–15 HCSB

The Big Picture

Simon Peter was by the shores of the Sea of Galilee—there in his hometown of Capernaum—when Jesus called him to be his disciple. Jesus said, "I will make you fishers of men!" (Matthew 4:19 HCSB), and Peter and his brother Andrew laid down their fishing nets and followed him. Peter had always been a laborer doing the backbreaking work of a net fisherman with his father and brother. There was something about his personality, however—a fiery temperament, a natural ability to lead—that suggested Peter was destined for something bigger. That destiny came into focus in the person of Jesus. Sure, Peter still had his hang-ups. But Jesus took Peter's natural traits and transformed him into a powerhouse for God.

Peter and the other disciples traveled with Jesus all over the region of Galilee across the Jordan into the region known as Decapolis, and down to Jerusalem. Peter saw some incredible things during that time. He heard Jesus preaching the incredible news of the kingdom of God, a whole new way of thinking about the world. He saw Jesus perform miracle after miracle. He saw lame people walk, blind people see, sick people get well again. It was like a whole new world opening up for Peter. People came from everywhere—from as far away as Syria—to be healed, to hear what Jesus was saying. Peter must have felt like a rock star—or at least a member of a rock star's posse.

But it was always somebody else who was getting healed—somebody else's son or daughter, somebody else's mother or father. When Jesus and his entourage returned to Peter's hometown of Capernaum, however, Peter saw things from a different perspective. His mother-in-law was at his house, sick in bed with a fever. You wonder if Peter felt a twinge of guilt; he'd been traipsing all over the countryside with the great Healer, and meanwhile his mother-in-law lay sick in his own house, in need of healing.

When Jesus walked into Peter's house, he immediately sized up the situation. He touched Peter's mother-in-law, and the fever went away. She got up and began to serve Jesus; she was her old self again, waiting on others rather than being waited on. For Peter, everything had come full circle. All that incredible power he had witnessed on the road with Jesus was relevant for him, too—under his roof, within his family.

The service of the less gifted brother is as pure as the service of the more gifted, and God accepts both with equal pleasure.

A. W. Tozer

"She got up and began to serve Him." That's a fascinating little detail. On the one hand, it's an indication of how fully Peter's mother-in-law was healed. No longer did she need to be looked after; she was well enough to look after other people. But isn't it interesting that that's what she chose to do? She didn't run outside to stretch her legs and get a breath of fresh air after her confinement. She didn't go next door to report to the neighbors: "He just touched me, and I felt better, just like that. . . . My son-in-law Peter is one of his best friends, you know. . . . And to think, I thought he wasn't good enough for my daughter. . . ."

No, she got up immediately and started serving Jesus. Gratitude toward her Healer motivated her to give back to him. She didn't waste any time. Jesus would only be there a short while. Peter's mother-in-law might have said, "While I've got you here, could you have a look at my back, too? It's been giving me fits." Instead, she said, "While I've got you here, let me serve you. I don't want to miss this once-in a-lifetime opportunity to serve the Son of God."

> *Whoever serves must do so with the strength that God supplies, so that God may be glorified in all things.*
>
> 1 Peter 4:11 NRSV

If you have received Christ, he has done a work of incredible healing in your life, healing that is even more incredible than what he did for Peter's mother-in-law. In that case, he was healing a sick person. In the work of salvation, Jesus is healing a dead person! Once "dead in your trespasses and sins" (Ephesians 2:1 NASB), now you're "alive together with Christ" (2:5 NASB). So what's the right response to that kind of miracle? Peter's mother-in-law got it right: you get up and start serving the One who healed you.

You do that by serving other people, imitating Jesus by putting other people's needs ahead of your own. When you're sick, it's really hard to do that. Sick people need to be served; they don't have a lot left over to give to others. But as God heals you more and more, you have more of yourself to give. Like Peter's mother-in-law, you can jump out of the sickbed and start serving.

When God blesses you, it's not all about you. He blesses you so you can be a blessing to other people. God is building a kingdom. You might think of it as contagious wellness spreading throughout the world.

In the kingdom of God, service is not a stepping-stone to nobility. It is nobility, the only kind of nobility that is recognized.

T. W. Manson

Albert Schweitzer achieved fame for his humanitarian work in Africa. But he never lost sight of the importance of the not-so-famous faithful:

"Always keep your eyes open for the little task, because it is the little task that is important to Jesus Christ. The future of the kingdom of God does not depend on the enthusiasm of this or that powerful person; those great ones are necessary too, but it is equally necessary to have a great number of little people who will do a little thing in the service of Christ."

Corrie ten Boom was a Christian who almost lost her life in a Nazi concentration camp, thanks to her service to her Jewish neighbors. Even in the concentration camp, she and her sister continued to love and serve those around them. Corrie's sister died, but Corrie survived to write some of the best inspirational books of the twentieth century. She told this story in one of her books:

"A visitor saw a nurse attending the sores of a leprosy patient. 'I would not do that for a million dollars,' she said. The nurse answered, 'Neither would I, but I do it for Jesus for nothing.'"

Zooming **In**

Peter seems to have come from a pretty close-knit family. He worked in the family fishing business with his father and brother. He lived with his family too. In Jesus' day, a couple would often live with the husband's family, after they got married. So what was Peter's mother-in-law doing at his house? Maybe she was a widow. In that day and age, it was hard for widows to provide for themselves. It wouldn't be surprising for a widow to move in with her daughter and son-in-law, even if they lived with her son-in-law's family. It's also possible that she was keeping her daughter company while Peter was out traveling with Jesus.

Peter learned two important things from the miraculous healing of his mother-in-law. First, he learned that the miracles of Jesus were meant for him and his family, not just others. Second, he learned the proper response to Jesus' healing: grateful service. What do you learn from this miracle?

God is doing great things all the time, even if they aren't as spectacular as the healing of Peter's mother-in-law. What great works of God have you seen firsthand?

Gratitude to God leads to service to God. How can you serve to show God your gratitude?

Sometimes you have to be healed before you can get up and serve. Is there something you need to be healed of before you can have anything to give? If so, what is it? If not, are you taking advantage of your health and wholeness to serve God and others?

A Dangerous Homecoming

*When they heard these things, all in the synagogue were
filled with wrath. And they rose up and drove him out of
the town and brought him to the brow of the hill on which
their town was built, so that they could throw him down
the cliff. But passing through their midst, he went away.*

Luke 4:28–30 ESV

**The
Big Picture**

When Jesus came back to his hometown of
Nazareth, his reputation preceded him. He had been
preaching and healing all over Judea and Galilee, and
he had been much acclaimed. He went to the synagogue in Nazareth, as was his custom any time he
arrived in a town, and there he taught from the
Scriptures. He read a passage about the Messiah from
the book of Isaiah, and then he told the people: "Today this Scripture has
been fulfilled in your hearing" (Luke 4:21 NASB). The people were amazed.
This was his hometown, after all, and many of the people surely remembered him from his boyhood there. They asked, "Is this not Joseph's son?"
(Luke 4:22 NASB).

There are two ways to look at that question. On the one hand, it could be
just town pride in a local boy made good—"Can you believe this is Joseph's
son making such a splash?" On the other hand, it could be an expression of
doubt: "How can this Jesus be the Messiah from God? We know he came
from right here in Nazareth. He's just Joseph's son." The second choice

seems more likely from Jesus' reaction. Jesus was never one to smooth over a conflict or an uncomfortable situation. He was more likely to bring a conflict to a head so it could be dealt with. That's what he did in this situation. He said, "No doubt you will quote this proverb to Me, 'Physician, heal yourself!'" (Luke 4:23 NASB). In other words, if Jesus can do great miracles in Capernaum, why won't he put on a show for the home folks? But Jesus refused to do any miracles. "No prophet is welcome in his hometown" (Luke 4:24 NASB), he observed. He offered up the Old Testament prophets Elijah and Elisha as examples. They healed foreigners instead of people in their own hometowns.

So on the one hand Jesus had townspeople pressing him to do miracles to prove he really was the Messiah (or maybe just to entertain them), and on the other hand he had townspeople who never would believe he was the Messiah because they didn't think the son of a simple carpenter could be the Messiah. He refused to appease either side.

And so, predictably, the people of Nazareth grew furious. So furious, in fact, that they drove Jesus out of town and to a cliff where they intended to throw him off. But somehow Jesus slipped through the crowd and got away. His work on earth wasn't finished yet.

Do your utmost to guard your heart,
for out of it comes life.

John Flavel

Take a closer look at that narrow escape. It's no huge surprise that Jesus got away from the murderous mob. He was the all-powerful God in the flesh, after all. No mob, no matter how big, could catch him if he didn't want to be caught. The Bible doesn't make it clear whether there was something supernatural about Jesus' disappearing act, or whether it was just the force of his personality that kept people from grabbing him. In any case, it is clear that Jesus was in total control of the situation.

Which brings up one question: if Jesus was in total control, why did he let things go so far? Why didn't he just say, "I'm outta here" the minute he realized that the old home folks weren't that into him anymore? He let them drive him to the cliff's edge because he wanted them to see what their hearts were capable of. He came to be the Savior—their Savior—and they needed to see how badly they needed one.

As Jesus slipped away, the people understood the darkness of their own hearts, but they also saw that Jesus was in control. He wouldn't let wickedness win the day.

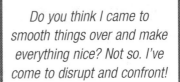

> *Do you think I came to smooth things over and make everything nice? Not so. I've come to disrupt and confront!*
>
> Luke 12:51 MSG

Sovereignty is the big theological word for the fact that God is totally in control. Christians believe that God is sovereign, that he does whatever he wants to do. But if God is sovereign over your life, why do you sometimes do bad things? Why doesn't God stop you from doing things that hurt you or other people?

Apply It
to Your Life

God is not interested in building a kingdom of robots. Yes, he could make everybody do exactly the right thing all the time. But he wants to be in relationship with people who are able to make choices—and who choose to seek God more and more. That means you will sometimes make the wrong choices. So what do you do then?

You feel bad when you sin. You're supposed to feel bad. But you're not supposed to be full of despair. Every time you sin, you get a glimpse of what your heart is capable of. You get a glimpse of what your Savior has saved you from. Celebrate the truth that God is bigger than all that. He may let you live with the consequences of bad choices, but ultimately he won't be overruled by sin.

Why then did God give them free will? Because free will, though it makes evil possible, is also the only thing that makes possible any love or goodness or joy worth having.

C. S. Lewis

R. T. France reflects on the story of Jesus in his hometown in *Jesus the Radical: A Portrait of the Man They Crucified*:

"Whatever Jesus was, he was not ordinary. He provoked extreme reactions, whether of acceptance or of rejection. One moment they were all on his side, the next they were trying to lynch him. And yet such was the authority of this extraordinary man that apparently he simply walked through a murderous crowd, and nobody laid a finger on him."

Robert P. Lockwood examines Jesus' visit to Nazareth in *A Faith for Grownups*. The "boys from the hometown" are scandalized by Jesus' claim that he is the fulfillment of all their hopes:

"The message that comes to us in this narrative is that Jesus isn't just that swell fellow, that friendly uncle. He is the Promised One of God, the Messiah. The revelation of God will be in him and to us, and our lives can never be the same."

Zooming **In**

Nazareth was a tiny and remote village—so tiny, in fact, that it wasn't even included in the list of forty-five cities of Galilee written by the first-century Jewish historian Josephus, or even in the list of sixty-three Galilean villages in the Jewish Talmud. The fact that the disciple Nathaniel asked, "Can any good thing come out of Nazareth?" (John 1:46 NASB) gives you some idea of how insignificant the village was. In a place that small, everybody probably knew everybody. Those weren't strangers trying to throw Jesus off the cliff. They were old friends. Some of them no doubt were related to Jesus.

Jesus allowed the people of Nazareth to get a look at what they were capable of. That's tough love. Human beings have a habit of overestimating their own goodness. But if people don't realize they need a Savior, they never reach out to him. How much do you need a Savior?

Write about a recent time you got a glimpse of your own heart. What did it look like?

_____

_____

_____

_____

What is the difference between feeling convicted of sin and feeling condemned? Which feeling motivates you to do better?

_____

_____

_____

_____

Think about God's sovereignty—his awesome control—and your ability to choose. How do you see these two seemingly contradictory forces working in your life?

_____

_____

_____

Honor to the Humble

> *Then Jesus came from Galilee to John at the Jordan, to be baptized by [John the Baptist]. But John tried to stop Him, saying, "I need to be baptized by You, and yet You come to me?"*
>
> Matthew 3:13–14 HCSB

The Big Picture

John the Baptist had quite a following. Even out in the desert, he got a lot of attention with that very short signature sermon of his: "Repent, for the kingdom of God is at hand" (Matthew 3:2 NASB). He said he was preparing the way for One who was greater than he. People could see there was something special about this John the Baptist. Some wondered if he was the prophet Elijah come back to earth. Perhaps some wondered if this wild man, this eater of bugs, might himself be the Messiah. But John didn't allow himself to be flattered by their good opinion. He was just the opening act: the real star of the show would soon be there. John said, "He who is coming after me is mightier than I, and I am not fit to remove His sandals" (Matthew 3:11 NASB). As John said, he only baptized with water, but the Messiah would baptize with the Holy Spirit and with fire.

Imagine John's surprise, then, when the Messiah showed up at the river Jordan and asked John to baptize him! John refused at first. "I need to be baptized by You," he said, "and yet You come to me?" John the Baptist spent his days getting other people to think about their need to repent. But he never lost sight of the fact that he, too, needed a Savior. He always said he was just pointing the way to the Messiah, not trying to promote himself. When it came down to it, he put his money where his mouth was. He was truly humbled by Jesus' request to be baptized.

But Jesus insisted. It was all part of God's plan, he said. So John baptized Jesus after all. And when Jesus came up out of the water, the skies opened up, and the Spirit of God came down in the shape of a dove. And God's voice came booming down: "This is My beloved Son, in whom I am well-pleased" (Matthew 3:17 NASB).

Just as he had said he would, John the Baptist paved the way for Jesus. "He must increase," John said, "but I must decrease" (John 3:30 NASB). There at the river, his desire was fulfilled. Of all the baptisms John performed, surely that one was the most exhilarating—the one he thought he was unworthy to perform.

Without humility of heart all the other virtues by which one runs toward God seem—and are—absolutely worthless.

Angela of Foligno

It's easy to see John's humility in his reluctance to baptize Jesus. "You should be baptizing *me*," he said, and he was right. Not even a great prophet like John the Baptist is too good to need the cleansing work of Jesus. But when you think about it, John's act of baptizing Jesus took some humility, too. John probably didn't understand why Jesus wanted to be baptized. Jesus certainly didn't have any sins to repent of. Normally John got to be the one who decided who got baptized and who didn't. But when Jesus came along, John submitted to his authority. "You want me to baptize you? All right, then, you're the boss." John gave his opinion, but when Jesus overruled him, he didn't argue any further. He simply obeyed.

The Bible makes it clear that God exalts the humble, not the proud. John the Baptist steadfastly refused to exalt himself. His humility was rewarded with the honor of baptizing the very Son of God. Was John worthy of such an honor? John didn't seem to think so. But Jesus did, and his opinion was the only one that mattered. It seems strange, but John showed real humility in receiving that honor.

> *Before destruction one's heart is haughty, but humility goes before honor.*
>
> Proverbs 18:12 NRSV

Humility is an important part of a life that pleases God. God exalts those who refuse to exalt themselves. He supports those who recognize that they need his support and can't do everything on their own. But humility doesn't have anything to do with feeling bad about yourself. You probably have days (maybe weeks, even months) when you

Apply It
to Your Life

think, *I'll never amount to anything. I'm a total loser*. That's not humility; that's low self-esteem. Humility says, "I'm not perfect—not even close—but God can do great things, even through somebody like me."

God has an incredible plan for your life. He has a whole lot of things for you to accomplish for his kingdom. A humble heart says, "Who, me? Who am I to do great things for God?" But that same humble heart says, "God, you're the boss, not me. And if you say you've got a great plan for me, who am I to deny it?" A poor self-image paralyzes you, keeps you from laying hold of God's great purposes and his great blessings. True humility frees you to follow God's plan. And in the process, you'll see incredible things.

Humility is to make a right estimate of one's self; it is no humility for a man to think less of himself than he ought.

C. H. Spurgeon

François Fénelon, a French bishop, pointed out that it is humility that makes a person nice to be around:

"There is no true and constant gentleness without humility. While we are so fond of ourselves, we are easily offended with others. Let us be persuaded that nothing is due to us, and then nothing will disturb us. Let us often think of our own infirmities, and we will become indulgent toward those of others."

Catherine Booth points out that false humility can turn into disobedience:

"I am tired of hearing the words, 'I can't.' Jeremiah said, 'I am a child'; but the Lord didn't pat him on the back and say, 'Jeremiah, that is very good, I like that in you; your humility is beautiful.' Oh no! God didn't want any such mock humility.

"He reproved and rebuked it. I do not like the humility that is too humble to do as it is bid. When my children are too humble to do as they are bid, I pretty soon find a way to make them. I say, 'Go and do it!' The Lord wants us to 'go and do it.'"

Zooming In

Though the baptisms performed by John are the first time the word *baptize* is used in the Bible, John didn't invent the practice. The Jews already had water purification rituals in place before John came along. There are many places in the Old Testament that mention God's people washing for religious purposes.

The word *humility* comes from the Latin word *humus*, meaning "dirt" or "earth." To be humble is to remain down-to-earth. You might say it means remembering that God made all of us out of dirt—a humble substance indeed, but one that was shaped and molded by God himself.

True humility has nothing to do with diminishing yourself to be less than you really are. It's about seeing your true and proper stature in light of the greatness of God. When you get a good look at God's greatness, you honor him. And God honors those who honor him.

Through the Eyes of Your Heart

 What are the dangers of overestimating your own importance?

_____

_____

_____

_____

 What are the dangers of underestimating your own importance?

_____

_____

_____

_____

 God exalts the humble. How does that work? Does being exalted by God disqualify you from the ranks of the humble?

_____

_____

_____

_____

A Burning Self-Righteousness

He sent some messengers on ahead to a Samaritan village to get things ready for him. But he was on his way to Jerusalem, so the people there refused to welcome him. When the disciples James and John saw what was happening, they asked, "Lord, do you want us to call down fire from heaven to destroy these people?" But Jesus turned and corrected them for what they had said.

Luke 9:52–55 CEV

The Big Picture

The Jews and the Samaritans weren't the best of friends. The Samaritans were what you might call lapsed Jews. At one time they were Jews, but they left the faith and began living more or less like the other pagans in that region. In the eyes of the Jews, that made the Samaritans worse than regular pagans. The Samaritans should have known better. The Samaritans were so "unclean," in fact, that "good" Jews refused to set foot in Samaria. The straightest shot from Jerusalem in the south to Jesus' home region of Galilee in the north ran straight through Samaria. But Jews traveling that way frequently went far out of their way to circle around Samaria, so they wouldn't become contaminated. Even a few miles out of their way meant a lot of extra effort because travelers in those days walked everywhere they went. But in the Jews' minds, it was better to have a few extra blisters than to have to deal with Samaritans. There was also a safety issue. Samaria had a reputation (probably earned) for being a pretty rough neighborhood.

Jesus, as you might expect, didn't put much stock in the Jews' anti-Samaritan prejudice. One of his most famous parables, after all, was of the good Samaritan. When he traveled between Galilee and Jerusalem, he took the straight route. He wasn't afraid to rub elbows with Samaritans, such as the woman at the well who was so surprised when a Jewish prophet spoke to her of Living Water (see John 4:5–42).

On one trip to Jerusalem, he sent messengers ahead to a Samaritan village to get things ready for him. But the people in the village refused to welcome him. James and John were furious. You can just picture them saying, "See, Jesus, we told you it was a bad idea to come through Samaria." They wanted to see a spectacular punishment for the loathsome Samaritans. They asked, "Lord, do you want us to call down fire from heaven to destroy these people?" Perhaps this incident is what inspired Jesus to give them their nickname—Boanerges, or "Sons of Thunder."

Jesus wouldn't let the Sons of Thunder bring thunder down on anybody. He corrected them: they obviously didn't understand what sort of work they were supposedly helping him with. He didn't come to destroy people's lives, Jesus said. He came to save them.

The man who is furthest from God is the man who thanks God he is not like the others.

William Barclay

Why do you think James and John were so eager to call down fire and destroy the Samaritan villagers? If you asked, they would probably have told you it was because the Samaritans had disrespected Jesus. They would probably even believe it. They had Jesus' back for sure. But that brings up the question, why didn't they offer to call down fire on everybody else who rejected Jesus? Jesus' home village of Nazareth not only rejected him, but tried to throw him off a cliff. James and John never offered to blow up Nazareth. This time, however, it was Samaritans—not Jews—who rejected Jesus. James and John already despised the Samaritans, long before any of this happened. They saw the Samaritans' lack of hospitality as an excuse for doing what they would have liked to do long before. And they could dress it up in a cloak of righteousness: "Hey, we're just looking out for Jesus—anybody want to pat us on the back?"

This is self-righteousness at its worst—not just an annoying, holier-than-thou attitude, but a cover for genuine wrongdoing in the name of Jesus. But Jesus won't have any part of it.

> Jesus said to them, "It is not those who are healthy who need a physician, but those who are sick; I did not come to call the righteous, but sinners."
>
> Mark 2:17 NASB

The story of James and John and the Samaritan villagers is a reminder of how easily your motives can get off track. Sure, righteousness is your goal. But righteousness doesn't give you license to tell the unrighteous to drop dead. If you're serious about following after Christ, you will experience opposition from people who don't believe the way you do. But you aren't supposed to treat those people as enemies.

If you're really committed to Jesus, you'll treat all people—even the enemies of Jesus—the way Jesus would treat them. A surprising number of Christians don't get that. They hear an instructor teaching a view of the world's origins that doesn't square with the Creation story in the Bible, or they hear a classmate express an opinion that opposes Christian morality, and before you know it, the gloves are off. They go from good Christian to attack dog in about two seconds.

Jesus didn't come to destroy people's lives, but to save them. What message do people get from the way you treat them and talk to them? Do your words and actions point them toward life and salvation, or do people get the impression that you wouldn't mind seeing them drop dead?

Open sin kills thousands of souls. Self-righteousness kills tens of thousands.

J. C. Ryle

Martin Luther King addressed racial prejudice not just as a social or political evil, but as a true spiritual issue:

"I refuse to accept the view that mankind is so tragically bound to the starless midnight of racism and war that the bright daybreak of peace and brotherhood can never become reality. I believe that unarmed truth and unconditional love will have the final word."

Henry George Spaulding, author of *The Teachings of Jesus,* offers this comment on James and John's desire to blow up the Samaritans:

"They are not followers of the Prince of Peace and Friend of sinners. He came to destroy these deep-seated enmities between man and man; to uproot the hateful prejudices which divide men. . . . He showed men who were hostile to each other what was good in each, and bade them make the best of each other."

Zooming In

How did the Jews and Samaritans grow to hate each other so much? It goes back hundreds of years to before the time of Jesus. The ten tribes of the Northern Kingdom, called Israel, were defeated by the Assyrians around 730 BC. The Assyrians carried many of the leading citizens of Samaria into captivity, but many more people were left behind. These remaining Samaritans began to lose their cultural and religious identity. Two centuries later, the two tribes of the Southern Kingdom were carried into captivity in Babylonia. When they returned home seventy years later, they were amazed to find how completely the Samaritans had assimilated with their pagan neighbors.

Self-righteousness isn't just an annoying habit. It's very bad for your soul, and it can also result in real harm to other people. James and John were very willing to hurt the Samaritan villagers who offended them, and they thought they were perfectly right. Have you ever had similar feelings?

What are some of the real-world effects of people's using religion as a cover for acting on their own prejudices?

_____

_____

_____

_____

How do you react when you encounter people who openly oppose Christianity? How ought you to react to those people?

_____

_____

_____

_____

As a Christian, how should you react to other Christians who use their faith as a club to batter people who disagree with them?

_____

_____

_____

Very Big Claims

> *"Your father Abraham rejoiced to see My day, and he saw it and was glad." Then the Jews said to Him, "You are not yet fifty years old, and have You seen Abraham?" Jesus said to them, "Most assuredly, I say to you, before Abraham was, I AM."*
>
> John 8:56–58 NKJV

The Big Picture

The Jews of Jesus' day took great pride in their status as the descendants of Abraham. Centuries earlier, God had made a promise: he would make a great nation out of Abraham and bless him with descendants more numerous than the stars of the sky. The Jews were the proof that God was keeping his promise. In a way, the whole idea of Jewishness was summarized in the idea of being Abraham's descendants. The Jews were one big family, all deriving from the same source, all looking to the same place for ultimate authority: God's promise to their common ancestor.

But one day a descendant of Abraham came along and reminded everyone that the true Father wasn't Abraham, but Abraham's Father—God himself. Jesus' countrymen thought they had God all figured out. But Jesus blew their minds. "If you were children of Abraham, you would follow his good example. I told you the truth I heard from God, but you are trying to kill me. Abraham wouldn't do a thing like that" (John 8:39–40 NLT).

The religious leaders seemed to know where Jesus was going with this conversation, so they tried to beat him to the punch: "'Don't accuse us of having someone else as our father!' they said. 'We just have one father, and he is God'" (John 8:41 cev). That sounded good, but Jesus shot back, "If God were your Father, you would love me, because I have come to you from God" (8:42 nlt). No, Jesus continued, their father must be the devil; that's who these people were acting like.

The Jews were pretty mad by now. "Just who do you think you are?" they asked, for by now they were catching on to the fact that Jesus was claiming to be greater than Abraham. Jesus kept pushing. "If I were simply honoring myself, that wouldn't mean anything. But my Father, God himself, honors me" (John 8:54, paraphrase). Then he said something very surprising: "Your father Abraham rejoiced to see My day, and he saw it and was glad" (8:56 nkjv). The tension in the air must have broken slightly at that point. This Jesus was obviously a nutcase if he expected anybody to believe he and Abraham had ever met. "You are not yet fifty years old," the religious leaders said, "and have You seen Abraham?" (8:57 nkjv). Jesus answered, "Before Abraham was, I AM" (8:58 nkjv). When they heard that answer, the people's mild amusement with a crazy man turned into a murderous rage. They picked up stones to stone Jesus to death. But Jesus slipped away.

No founder of any religion has dared to claim for himself one fraction of the assertions made by the Lord Jesus Christ about himself.

Henry J. Heydt

Take a closer look at Jesus' answer to the taunts of his enemies. He had said some pretty hard things to these people. He even went so far as to call them the spawn of Satan. But all those perceived insults weren't what really set them off. What made them pick up stones to kill him was that little sentence, "Before Abraham was, I AM." It's an odd thing to say, of course, but what's the big deal? The big deal is that Jesus is equating himself with God. When God spoke to Moses from the burning bush, Moses asked his name, and God answered, "I AM THAT I AM" (Exodus 3:14 KJV). When Jesus said, "Before Abraham was, I AM," he wasn't just claiming to be really old, nor was he making a grammatical error with his strange verb tense. He was actually claiming godhood.

If a mere mortal claims to be God, that's blasphemy. And blasphemy was punishable by death. That's why the people picked up stones. They thought they were doing the proper thing. They weren't ready to accept the outlandish idea that a carpenter's son from the obscure village of Nazareth could be God in the flesh.

In Christ the fullness of God lives in a human body.

Colossians 2:9 NLT

C. S. Lewis once observed that Jesus didn't leave you the option of believing that he was just a great man, or even just a great prophet. When a man claims to be God, either he's a liar, he's a crazy person, or he really is God. There's no half-hearted cop-out available. You can't say, "It really doesn't matter whether or not Jesus was truly God; the

Apply It
to Your Life

important thing is that he had cool ideas about loving your neighbor and stuff like that." No, he was always confrontational, and he always made people decide—lunatic, liar, or Savior?

When Jesus set himself up as being superior to Abraham, he was telling his hearers, "Listen—I'm making claims that go way beyond your culture—even the accepted religious culture." Culture shapes beliefs. But Jesus says, "Forget about what the culture says. What do *you* say about me?" Maybe you've grown up in a church culture, and the easy thing is to go with the flow: "Sure, I believe in Jesus. Why not?" But that passive acceptance doesn't please God. You have to come to terms with the claims of Jesus for yourself. Forget about what you're *supposed* to believe. You've got to decide: liar, lunatic, or Savior?

Christ's claims are either cosmic or comic.
John Blanchard

How Others **See It**

Here's a more complete version of C. S. Lewis's famous "liar, lunatic, or Lord" passage from *Mere Christianity*:

"A man who was merely a man and said the sort of things Jesus said would not be a great moral teacher. He would either be a lunatic—on a level with the man who says he is a poached egg—or else he would be the Devil of Hell. You must make your choice. Either this man was, and is, the Son of God: or else a madman or something worse."

Lest anyone should claim that Jesus never really said he was God, J. N. D. Anderson sums up the claims of Jesus:

"He said that he was in existence before Abraham and that he was 'lord' of the Sabbath; he claimed to forgive sins; he continually identified himself . . . with the one he termed his heavenly Father; he accepted men's worship. And he said that he was to be the judge of men at the last day."

Zooming **In**

YAHWEH, the Jewish name for God, is a form of "I AM," the name God spoke to Moses at the burning bush. The original pronunciation of the word has been lost, because the Jews were so respectful of the name of God that they were forbidden to speak it, choosing instead to call God *Adonai,* or "LORD." The name *JEHOVAH* is another version of *YAHWEH,* though the words sound very different. The word was spelled without vowels, YHWH. Y's and J's were interchangeable, as were W's and V's. So YHWH becomes JHVH. Plug in different vowels, and you get JeHoVaH instead of YaHWeH.

Everybody has to come to terms with the claims of Christ for himself or herself. Church, friends, even books like these can help you reach a conclusion, but in the end, you're accountable for your own beliefs. Journaling is a good way to think through what you believe.

What do you think of C. S. Lewis's "liar, lunatic, or Lord" quotation? Do you find it convincing? Do you think a nonbeliever would find it convincing? Why or why not?

Jesus asked Peter, "Who do you say I am?" (Luke 9:20 NLT). How would you answer that question?

Why does it matter whether or not Jesus was actually God? Why can't you just follow his good teachings and leave it at that?

Bold Witness

> *"Everyone in Israel should then know for certain that God has made Jesus both Lord and Christ, even though you put him to death on a cross." When the people heard this, they were very upset. They asked Peter and the other apostles, "Friends, what shall we do?"*
>
> Acts 2:36–37 CEV

The **Big Picture**

When Jesus finally ascended into heaven—forty days after he rose again from the grave—he promised his disciples that he would send the Holy Spirit to empower them to be his witnesses throughout the world. That promise was fulfilled about ten days later, at the Feast of Pentecost. All twelve disciples were in a room together, and a sound like the rushing of a great wind filled the place. Then a tongue of fire appeared above each disciple's head, and they were suddenly able to speak in different languages.

Because of the feast, Jerusalem was full of people from all over the known world—devout Jews who had come to celebrate the feast in their holiest city. When the disciples began to preach, the people were amazed to hear these uneducated working-class men speaking in languages they could understand.

Some of the hard-hearted in the crowd sneered, "They are drunk" (Acts 2:13 CEV)—though it would be a very strange drunkenness that makes a person suddenly able to speak or understand foreign languages. Peter stood up and told the people, no, what you see isn't public drunkenness, but the fulfillment of what the prophet Joel wrote long ago: "I will pour out My Spirit on all humanity" (Joel 2:28 HCSB). He went on to recap the story of Jesus: he came to earth from God, he died, and he rose again in power. One of the surprising things about the sermon was Peter's aggressive, in-your-face approach toward his audience. He openly accused them of killing Jesus: "You used lawless people to nail him to a cross and kill him. . . . God has made this Jesus, whom you crucified, both Lord and Messiah" (author's paraphrase).

It didn't seem like the best approach for winning friends and influencing people. But it worked. People responded to Peter's message. Instead of getting mad about Peter's accusations, the people were cut to the heart; they wanted to know what to do.

That day, about three thousand people joined the church. Their lives were totally changed. They devoted themselves to the teachings of Jesus and to fellowship and prayer. They sold their possessions and shared with the needy. The same Holy Spirit that empowered the disciples to speak in foreign languages now empowered these new Christians to live a completely different kind of life.

The Holy Spirit is not a blessing from God.
He is God.

Colin Urquhart

The apostles showed real boldness when they stood before the people gathered at Pentecost. But they hadn't always been so bold. After Jesus died, and even after he rose again, the twelve apostles were scared and confused. Some of them had wandered back to their old jobs on the fishing boats, apparently unsure what else to do with their time. The apostle Peter, you will remember, went so far as to deny that he even knew Jesus on the night before Jesus was crucified. That was less than two months earlier. Now he was preaching to a huge crowd, making thousands of converts.

What was the difference? The Holy Spirit. The Holy Spirit turned the apostles from cowards into incredibly bold witnesses. Notice also the contents of Peter's message. It was very straightforward, very simple; it didn't start out with a joke and end with a strong emotional appeal. It didn't follow the rules you learn in speech class. In fact, it seemed calculated to offend rather than attract. And yet three thousand people joined the church that day. That was obviously the work of the Holy Spirit, who doesn't depend on eloquence to get the job done.

The Spirit searches everything, even the depths of God.

1 Corinthians 2:10 NRSV

Like the twelve apostles, you are called to be a bold witness. It's a scary thing to think about, taking a public stand for Jesus. It was scary to the apostles, too. It helps to remember that if you're in Christ, the same Spirit that empowered and motivated the apostles lives in you also.

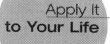

Apply It to Your Life

Here's another thing to remember: the work of the Holy Spirit doesn't depend on your ability to say exactly the right thing. No, the important thing is for you to make yourself available, to be willing to try. Who knows what's going to make a difference in a person's life? At Pentecost, the apostles just opened their mouths, and the right words came out. People heard what God needed them to hear, even if it was in a foreign language. There's nothing all that impressive about Peter's sermon as recorded in Acts 2. But it was exactly what the people needed to hear. It made them ask the question, "What do we need to do?" Being an effective witness doesn't all come down to your persuasive skill. You can be bold in the knowledge that it's the Holy Spirit who's at work when you tell other people about God.

We do not need to wait for the Holy Spirit to come: he came on the day of Pentecost. He has never left the church.

John Stott

Here is what Cyril of Alexandria, one of the early church fathers, had to say about the Holy Spirit.

"All of us who have received one and the same Spirit, that is, the Holy Spirit, are in a sense blended together with one another and with God. . . . The one and undivided Spirit of God, who dwells in all, leads all into spiritual unity."

A.W. Tozer had this to say about the Holy Spirit:

"Spell this out in capital letters: THE HOLY SPIRIT IS A PERSON. He is not enthusiasm. He is not courage. He is not energy. He is not the personification of all good qualities, like Jack Frost is the personification of cold weather. Actually, the Holy Spirit is not the personification of anything. He is a Person, the same as you are a person."

Zooming **In**

The Jews were some of the most experienced travelers in all the Roman Empire. Acts 2 gives a list of the countries of origin of the Jews who had traveled to celebrate Pentecost in Jerusalem. People had come from modern-day Iran, Iraq, Turkey, Egypt, Libya, Crete, and Arabia, not to mention the countries right around Palestine.

The big word for "speaking in tongues" is *glossolalia*. Glossolalia is still practiced in some churches, where it is considered a sign of the presence of the Holy Spirit. These churches, which place emphasis on the more visible signs of the Holy Spirit, are often known as "Pentecostal" churches. They derive that name from the Feast of Pentecost as described in Acts 2, where the Spirit was exhibited in spectacular ways.

The stories of the Holy Spirit's work in the book of Acts are amazing. What's even more amazing is the realization that every Christian has that same Spirit living inside. If you're in Christ, you have huge, tremendous power hidden in you. Are you ready to turn it loose?

Through the Eyes of Your Heart

People talk about God the Father and God the Son a lot more than they talk about God the Spirit. Why do you think that is?

_____

_____

_____

Does anything hold you back from talking boldly about Christ in your school or other social settings? Does it change things to know that the Holy Spirit is really the One doing the work? Why or why not?

_____

_____

_____

At Pentecost, the Holy Spirit broke down language barriers that would have hindered people's ability to receive the gospel. Among people you know, what kind of barriers affect their ability to receive the gospel? How can the Holy Spirit break down those barriers?

_____

_____

_____

Future Glory

The Big Picture

Never a dull moment. The apostle Paul lived through some pretty intense times in the course of his career. When Stephen, the first Christian martyr, was stoned to death, young Saul (as Paul was originally known) held the coats of the people who threw the stones. He later took a more active role in the persecution of the church. Little did he know that he would soon be on the receiving end of that same persecution. After a spectacular conversion to Christianity, the great enemy of the church became one of its greatest champions. For the rest of his life, he was called upon many times to put his money where his mouth was.

In Damascus Paul had to make a daring escape—lowered in a basket through a hole in the city wall—to get away from religious leaders who were plotting to murder him. In Lystra the people stoned him and dragged his limp body out of the city, supposing him to be dead. But he survived and continued his missionary journey. A big fight with his friend Barnabas may have been just as traumatic. In Thyatira he was beaten and thrown into prison

take a **CLOSER** look for teens

with Silas, then rescued by an angel and an earthquake. In Thessalonica he escaped a riot.

Paul had already experienced all that (and would eventually experience much more, including shipwreck, snakebite, and his own martyrdom) when he wrote, "I consider that the sufferings of this present time are not worth comparing with the glory that is to be revealed to us." Paul wasn't just talking. He knew what suffering was. Yet he refused to allow his life to be defined by suffering. He could have easily looked at all that hardship and said, "Oh, what's the use? I try to serve God, and all I get is trouble in return!" Surely he could have found a job that wouldn't involve getting stoned and beaten and imprisoned. But Paul understood that an easy life wasn't what he wanted. He considered all that hardship a small price to pay for the privilege of helping to build the kingdom of God. No earthly glory could compare to that glory. No earthly comfort could compare to the comfort of knowing that he was being obedient to God.

Godliness is glory in the seed,
and glory is godliness in the flower.

Thomas Watson

Take a Closer Look

Take a closer look at Paul's idea of future glory. The book of Revelation speaks not only of a new heaven, but also a new earth. In this passage, Paul is obviously thinking of that new earth. He speaks of creation longing to be set free from the futility to which it has been subjected. In other words, the things of earth aren't just going to vaporize at the end of time; they're going to be redeemed, restored to what God meant them to be. A new earth—a perfected earth. That's what you have to look forward to. That's something worth working for, even suffering for.

When Paul was suffering for the gospel, he wasn't just trying to rescue human souls so they could someday fly away to live in heaven in some disembodied state. Paul's work was to participate in God's plan for *all* creation. The kingdom of God isn't just about souls. It starts there, yes, but as people are changed from the inside out, they help to change the world around them. The whole world belongs to God, and one of these days he's going to set everything right again, on earth as it is in heaven.

> [Jesus speaking:] The glory which You have given Me I have given to them.
>
> John 17:22 NASB

You've probably never been in a shipwreck. You've probably never been imprisoned for your faith or dragged out and stoned. But you still know a thing or two about suffering. You live in a world where things don't always work out the way they're supposed to. You fail exams. You get zits. Sometimes it gets worse than that. Relationships

fall apart. People you love get sick and die. You experience persecution when you stand up for what you believe in. That's just part of the deal when you live in the middle of a creation that has been "subjected to futility" (Romans 8:20 ESV), as the apostle Paul put it.

But that doesn't mean everything is futile. All those sufferings, all those indignities don't seem quite so big if you can make yourself see them in light of the greater glory that is your destiny. If all you see is this life, it's very tempting to say, "Oh, forget it! Why should I look out for anybody but myself? The world sure isn't looking out for me." Why be self-controlled? Why not grab at every little pleasure that offers itself up? Because you're looking for something much greater. You're looking for the glory of a new heaven and a new earth.

Look at everything as though you were seeing it for the first time or the last time. Then your time on earth will be filled with glory.

Betty Smith

How Others See It

In C. S. Lewis's *The Voyage of the Dawn Treader,* the ship *Dawn Treader* sails through a sea of glory. Jonathan Rogers comments on Lewis's idea of glory in this passage from *The World According to Narnia*:

"We do not merely want to see beauty. . . . We want something else which can hardly be put into words—to be united with the beauty we see, to pass into it, to receive it into ourselves, to bathe in it, to become part of it. On earth we are always outside the beauty we observe. The glory of heaven is to shine with the same beauty that breaks our hearts on earth. Glory in the biblical sense isn't merely brightness; it's the brightness of honor, of accolade, of good report. . . . The truest and highest honor is the approbation of the Judge of Heaven and Earth: 'Well done, good and faithful servant!' (Matthew 25:21 NIV). To bask in God's approval—it may sound like the ultimate vanity. But as Lewis argues, it is the purest, even the humblest pleasure of the creature, to please the One who created you for his Pleasure."

Zooming In

The Greek word translated as "glory" in the New Testament is *doxa,* from the word *dokeo,* "to seem." As Vine's *Expository Dictionary of New Testament Words* puts it, *doxa* "signifies an opinion, estimate, and hence the honor resulting from a good opinion." To give God glory is to give others (and yourself) reason to hold God in a higher opinion. On the flip side, to say that believers look forward to glory is to say that it is their destiny to share in that honor themselves. In heaven, believers become glorious by reflecting God's glory. They become beautiful by reflecting God's beauty. If you are in Christ, that's your destiny.

You live in an imperfect world. That's just the way it is. But that's not the way it's always going to be. As Paul says, the tough things you go through in this life are going to seem as light as a feather once you get a look at the glory that awaits you.

You're young. Most people your age have a long life ahead of them. What's the point of pondering future glory?

_____

_____

_____

_____

If future glory involves a new heaven *and* a new earth—in other words, if it's not all about flying away to heaven as a spirit—does that change the way you think about the world you live in?

_____

_____

_____

What kind of mistakes can you make by failing to think about future glory— by paying too much attention to the difficulties and disappointments of *this* life?

_____

_____

_____

_____

The Perfect Job

> *The LORD made a garden in a place called Eden, which was in the east, and he put the man there. The LORD God placed all kinds of beautiful trees and fruit trees in the garden. . . . The LORD God put the man in the Garden of Eden to take care of it and to look after it.*
>
> Genesis 2:8–9, 15 CEV

The Big Picture

Nobody else has ever had it so good. Adam and Eve lived in an earthly paradise, where the fruit of every tree (except one) was theirs for the taking—where there were no thorns or thistles, only the lush bounty of the earth. Their job was to tend the garden. It was pleasant work, meaningful work. The fact that they did their work without any clothes on suggests that they didn't even have to worry about mosquitoes.

You already know what happened next. The serpent deceived Eve, and she ate from that one tree God had forbidden them to eat from. Adam followed suit, and you might say all hell broke loose in their earthly paradise. Gods' punishment was swift: "By the sweat of your brow you will eat your food" (Genesis 3:19 NIV), he said. There was no more free lunch. Suddenly Adam and Eve were no longer working in cooperation with the earth; in a sense they were working against it. The good plants faced competition from thorns and weeds, and it took a lot of hard work to help the fruit trees bear the fruit that they had once yielded so freely. The sun sometimes shone too hot now, and sometimes the winters got too cold. Naked gardening was out of the question now, not only because of the swarms of mosquitoes, but also because Adam and Even felt ashamed of their nakedness. Everything was out of whack.

Paradise was lost. Adam and Eve now lived in a world like the one you live in, where things are always breaking down, where it takes a lot of hard work to make any good thing last.

But God didn't abandon Adam and Eve. He made a garment to cover their nakedness and shame. More important, he promised to send a Savior for Adam and Eve's descendants, One who would crush the head of the serpent who deceived Eve. They would still have to live with the results of their sin. Eve and her descendants would still experience pain in childbirth. Adam and his descendants would still have to sweat and struggle to make ends meet. But they could live and struggle in hope. And their work, even though it was hard, would not be in vain.

Diamonds are only chunks of coal that stuck to their jobs.

Minnie Richard Smith

**Take a
Closer Look**

"By the sweat of your brow . . ." (Genesis 3:19 NIV). You might already know that hot, sweaty, hard labor is the result of the Fall, part of God's punishment for Adam and Eve's sin. There's no easy way to get by in the world. But a lot of people don't realize that Adam and Eve did work even before the Fall. Genesis 2:15 says that God put Adam in the Garden of Eden "to cultivate it and keep it" (NASB). From day one, human beings have had work they were responsible for. Work itself isn't a punishment; it's an essential part of what it means to be a human being. Sure, there is such a thing as degrading labor. But on the whole, labor is a good thing. Thanks to the Fall, work is more difficult than it should be. But it's still a whole lot better than laziness and idleness.

Work gives you a sense of purpose. That's not to say you should find your whole reason for living in a job. Rather, work is one important way—perhaps *the* most important way—that people serve God. The whole world belongs to God, and he grants everybody the privilege of caring for some little patch of it.

> *Whatever you do, work at it with all your heart, as working for the Lord, not for men.*
>
> Colossians 3:23 NIV

Just as Adam had the responsibility to cultivate and keep the Garden of Eden, you are accountable for some little patch of the world. It may be the counter at the fast-food place where you work, or the pool where you lifeguard, or the yards you mow. Your little patch definitely includes your schoolwork. Whatever your job, it is a service to God when you work to make the most of your talents and time, and when you serve the people you work for and work with. Ultimately, God is the One you work for.

Apply It to Your Life

Yes, your work is often tedious. Schoolwork isn't always a blast, and neither are most of the jobs that students get. Here's a little secret: all jobs—even the best-paying jobs for the most highly educated professionals—are tedious and difficult at times. That's just what the world is like after the Fall. But that doesn't mean your work is meaningless, or that you shouldn't give it your all. Even if you lived in unfallen bliss, you'd still have work to do, because that has always been a part of God's plan for the human race. You'd better get to work!

All good work is done the way ants do things, little by little.
Lafcadio Hearn

In his book *The Cure for the Common Life,* Max Lucado has a lot to say about doing work that really matters. You probably haven't embarked on your career just yet, but now is as good a time as any to think about the importance of work:

"Whether you work at home or in the marketplace, your work matters to God. And your work matters to society. We need you! Cities need plumbers. Nations need soldiers. Stoplights break. Bones break. We need people to repair the first and set the second. Someone has to raise kids, raise cane, and manage the kids who raise Cain."

Sure, work after the Fall is often difficult, but George McDonald points out that not all work—not even all work worth doing—has to be difficult:

"Do you think the work God gives us to do is never easy? Jesus says His yoke is easy, His burden is light. People sometimes refuse to do God's work just because it is easy. This is sometimes because they cannot believe that easy work is His work."

Zooming **In**

In the phrase "to cultivate it and keep it" (Genesis 2:15 NASB), the Hebrew word translated "cultivate" is the same word translated elsewhere in the Old Testament as "serve"—as in, "serve God," or "serve in the Temple," or "serve a master." That puts Adam's everyday work—and your work, too—in a different perspective.

The word *vocation* is often used as a synonym for *job* or *career.* It actually comes from the Latin word *vocare,* "to call." Vocation literally means "calling." To view your work as a calling from God—even if your work right now is just getting through school—changes your whole outlook.

Through the
Eyes of
Your Heart

Think about your attitude toward work—schoolwork, part-time job, household chores, future career. Do you usually view work as a necessary evil? As a way to serve God? As drudgery? As your main purpose in life? How do you think your attitude matches up with a biblical view of work?

What do you consider your dream job? Why?

What has observing your parents taught you—true or false—about work?

A Towering Mistake

"Look!" [God] said. "If they can accomplish this when they have just begun to take advantage of their common language and political unity, just think of what they will do later. Nothing will be impossible for them! Come, let's go down and give them different languages. Then they won't be able to understand each other."

Genesis 11:6–7 NLT

The Big Picture

After the Great Flood, the next story in the Bible is that of the Tower of Babel. Noah's descendants apparently were reluctant to spread out. They all lived on a plain in Shinar, which is later known as Babylonia in present-day Iraq. Everybody spoke the same language—which makes sense when you think about it. They all came from the same place, and they all lived in the same place, so why wouldn't they speak the same language?

Somebody had the bright idea of building a huge tower that would reach all the way up to heaven. The tower would be in the middle of a great city, truly the center of the world. It would be their way of making a name for themselves. Just as important, they thought, it would be a way of keeping their single culture intact. The great city and the heaven-reaching tower would keep the people from scattering, they thought. If their architectural dream became a reality, why would anybody want to go anywhere else?

It sounds innocent enough. But God didn't see it that way. He looked down and saw a human race determined to make it on their own. In all their grand plans, they made no mention of the God who created them and who rescued their ancestors from the Flood. They seemed, in fact, determined to make God irrelevant. Their tower would raise them up to heaven, like gods themselves. They wanted to find their identity in their great civic project, not in their relationship with God. Their determination to make a name for themselves suggests they had no interest in exalting the name of God.

"Just think of what they will do later," God said. "Nothing will be impossible for them!" Though that may seem like a good situation—for a nation to be so powerful that nothing is impossible—it never works out. So God humbled the people of the plain. He confused their language so they couldn't understand one another. He scattered the people all over the earth. The construction project was abandoned. From then on, the place was called Babel, because of the babble of different languages that rose up there. The great variety of the world's languages and cultures came into being because of that seeming catastrophe.

Half the harm that is done in this world is due to people who want to feel important.

T. S. Eliot

A quick look at the story of Babel might leave you with the impression that God scattered the people and garbled their language because he didn't appreciate the competition to his authority. A closer look reveals that there's more to it than that. As has been discussed already, an all-powerful human government is never a good thing. Beyond that, however, there's the biblical command to "fill the earth" (Genesis 1:28 NLT). It was one of God's first commandments to the human race, and the people of the Shinar Plain were ignoring it, choosing instead to stay in one place and to stay as homogeneous as possible.

God's goal for humankind is to have people from every tribe and nation praising him in every language in the world—a brotherhood of very different people united under the Fatherhood of God. The people in this story were trying to do the opposite—creating and preserving a single culture that had no need of God. By scattering the people and confusing their language, God wasn't just punishing the people. He was making them do what they should have been doing already—spreading out, filling the earth, developing new cultures and new languages through which the greatness of God would be celebrated.

> Thus says the LORD: Do not let the wise boast in their wisdom, do not let the mighty boast in their might, do not let the wealthy boast in their wealth; but let those who boast boast in this, that they understand and know me, that I am the LORD.
>
> Jeremiah 9:23–24 NRSV

Whom do you picture when you hear the word *Christian*? If you're like most Christians, you picture somebody who looks a lot like you—somebody who speaks your language, wears your kind of clothes, likes your kind of music. But God makes it very clear that he's building a kingdom of people from all over the world. Yes, Americans have

an important part to play in God's kingdom, but our role is no more important than that of Africans or Asians or Arabs or Amazon tribesmen. Just look at Christians around the world. The church is on fire in Africa. Many of the world's largest Christian churches are in Korea. Latin America is a hotbed for the faith.

God is very big. No one culture is big enough to praise him fully. It takes all kinds of people raising their voices together even to begin to praise God. That doesn't only mean different nationalities and languages, but subcultures, too—urban, rural, suburban; skater dudes, jocks, brains; rich, poor, middle class. Christians don't have to try to erase all differences and become all alike. Rather, they can celebrate their differences, knowing that where it really matters, they're all on the same page.

Much of what passes for modern, western Christianity isn't of Jesus. We can (and do) lose Jesus right in the middle of prayer meetings and worship services.

Mike Erre

In *Genesis: Beginning and Blessing*, R. Kent Hughes has this to say about the builders of the Tower of Babel:

"The fact that they feared being scattered is proof that their fellowship with God and their unity with each other had been shattered by sin. . . . Their attempt to preserve their unity by outward means would not be successful apart from coercion, as world history so sadly proves. And here God would graciously work to effect their scattering."

German Theologian Erich Sauer saw the confusion of languages at Babel as not only a separation of one language into many, but also a fragmentation of human understanding and communication:

"The original language in which Adam in Paradise had named all the animals was, as it were, a great mirror in which the whole of nature was accurately reflected. But now God shattered this mirror, and each people retained only a fragment of it . . . and now each people sees only a piece of the whole, but never the whole completely."

Zooming **In**

The word *Babel* comes from the Hebrew word *balal*, which means "confusion." The word made its way into English as *babble*, meaning "to speak words or sounds indistinctly," or "to speak foolishly and/or incoherently." As a matter of fact, many languages throughout the world use some version of the word *Babel* to mean "confused" or "confusing talk."

Some people have suggested that the scattering of the people after the Tower of Babel was connected to continental drift—the idea that the seven continents were originally one land mass that broke up and separated. There's not much scholarly support for this connection, but it's interesting to ponder the possibility that God didn't just disperse the people, but also the ground they lived on!

The tower builders were trying to consolidate their power and create one huge culture that didn't need God. But that wasn't God's plan. He wanted his kingdom to consist of people of every color, speaking hundreds of languages. That truth should change the way you think about people who are different from you.

Do you tend to equate "Christian" with "American"? Why do you think that habit is so common among American Christians?

_____

_____

_____

_____

God said he would bring people to himself from every tribe and nation. What are the "tribes" at your school? Do you think God will bring people from each of those "tribes" into his kingdom? Why or why not?

_____

_____

_____

God was doing the tower builders a favor when he prevented them from being able to do exactly as they pleased. Write about a time when God did you a favor by preventing you from having your own way.

_____

_____

_____

False Fear, Blessed Boldness

The land we explored devours those living in it. All the people we saw there are of great size. We saw the Nephilim there (the descendants of Anak come from the Nephilim). We seemed like grasshoppers in our own eyes, and we looked the same to them.

Numbers 13:32–33 NIV

The Big Picture

The children of Israel had seen incredible things. They had seen the Nile River turned to blood, the sky black with locusts. They had seen the Angel of Death take the firstborn of the Egyptians yet pass over the houses of the Hebrews. They had seen the Red Sea split in two, and they had walked out of Egypt on dry ground. They saw the pursuing Egyptian army drowned as the waves crashed down on them. God had promised the Hebrews a land flowing with milk and honey, and so far he had proven himself faithful in some pretty spectacular ways.

The children of Israel were poised on the east side of the river Jordan, ready to push west into the land God had promised them. They had sent twelve spies ahead to scout the place out; now they were back, and the news wasn't good. Yes, the spies said, the land is a fruitful land, flowing with milk and honey, just as God had told them. What God didn't tell them was that the land was populated by a race of giants, the Nephilim. The cities were large and fortified. There was no way the ragtag Israelites could defeat them, the spies said.

One of the spies, by the name of Caleb, spoke up against the others. "We should go up and take possession of the land, for we can certainly do it" (Numbers 13:30 NIV). Caleb remembered what he had seen on the incredible journey out of Egypt. There was no earthly way the Israelites should have escaped from the Egyptians. But they did. And God would surely give them this land, just as he said he would.

But the other spies were insistent, according to Numbers 13:32. "The land we explored devours those living in it," they said. They had just gotten finished saying it was a land flowing with milk and honey (Numbers 13:27). But now it's a land that devours people. After getting a look at those giants, they said, "We were like grasshoppers in our own sight, and so we were in their sight" (13:33 NKJV). Their pessimistic view carried the day. Rather than invading the land that God had promised to them, the Israelites listened to their fears and hung back. As a result of their disobedience, the people of Israel had to wait another forty years to enter the Promised Land. That generation of people who were afraid to trust in God's protection died in the wilderness.

Courage is not the absence of fear,
but the mastery of fear.
Author Unknown

Take a closer look at the spies' comment that they looked like grasshoppers next to the giants in the Promised Land. "We became like grasshoppers *in our own sight.*" They had a major self-image problem. God had made them giant-slayers. That's what he saw when he looked at the Israelites. But they didn't see themselves that way. They saw themselves as grasshoppers to be crushed underfoot by the very people God had promised to place in their hands.

Caleb and Joshua shouted and jumped and waved their arms: "Forget about the giants! If God wants to give us this land, he can give us this land!" But nobody would listen. Notice that Joshua and Caleb never denied the fact that there were giants in the land. But they focused on a much more relevant fact: God was a whole lot bigger than any Nephilim, and God was on their side. The Israelites, however, weren't able to see things their way. They could only see the things that were visible to their eyes. Their short memories and their stunted imaginations didn't enable them to see that the unseen God was more real than the seen giants.

> *Be strong and courageous, for you shall give this people possession of the land which I swore to their fathers to give them.*
>
> Joshua 1:6 NASB

Fear can really mess up your perspective on things. You look at a challenge, and you start feeling about the size of a grasshopper. Fear always tries to convince you that you are just being realistic. "Face the facts for once. You're never going to overcome this thing. Can't you see that?" But fear isn't nearly as clear-eyed as it pretends to be.

It suffers from some serious distortions. The spies felt like grasshoppers next to the Nephilim. Does that sound realistic to you? The Nephilim were big men, but they weren't that big.

You deal with fear by making yourself get back to the things that you know to be absolutely true, even if you can't see them. It's always possible that your fear is realistic. In that case, be scared, by all means, but still trust God. Often, however, you find that fear invents its own things to be scared of. A land flowing with milk and honey becomes a land that devours its people in your frightened vision. A land promised by God becomes a land guarded by invincible giants. But you're a giant-slayer. God has plans to bless you and prosper you. Do you have the boldness to charge ahead?

Courage is the first of human qualities because it is the quality which guarantees all the others.

Winston Churchill

How Others
See It

Martin Luther King Jr., a man of tremendous courage, offered this contrast between courage and cowardice:

"Courage is an inner resolution to go forward in spite of obstacles and frightening situations; cowardice is a submissive surrender to circumstance.

"Courage breeds courageous self-affirmation; cowardice produces destructive self-abnegation.

"Courage faces fear and thereby masters it; cowardice represses fear and is thereby mastered by it. . . .

"We must constantly build dikes of courage to hold back the flood of fear."

Robert Louis Stevenson has fostered a sense of adventure and courage in generations of young readers through books such as *Treasure Island* and *Kidnapped*. Here's what he had to say about boldness:

"The world has no room for cowards. We must all be ready somehow to toil, to suffer, to die. And yours is not the less noble because no drum beats before you when you go out to your daily battlefields, and no crowds shout your coming when you return from your daily victory and defeat."

Zooming **In**

A whole generation died out during the forty years that God made the Israelites wander in the wilderness—everyone except those two faithful spies, Caleb and Joshua. They led the military conquest of Canaan. As a matter of fact, the book of Joshua tells of both Caleb and Joshua leading armies in victories over the Nephilim.

It is believed that the giant Goliath was one of the Nephilim mentioned in this passage. Goliath was one of a whole family of giants in the Philistine city of Gath. Besides being unusually large, the members of his family also had six fingers on each hand and six toes on each foot (see 2 Samuel 21:20 and 1 Chronicles 20:6).

For the Israelites, fear and forgetfulness were closely linked. If they had only remembered what God had done for them in the past, they wouldn't have been so fearful about the future. Everybody deals with fear. The question is, are you going to let fear define your life?

What are you afraid of? What is it that keeps you from living boldly and radically for God, enjoying the amazing life he offers you?

_____

_____

_____

_____

God has done great things in your life. Are you in the habit of remembering them? Make a list of the times when it was obvious that God was at work. Just thinking about those things can blast away your fear.

_____

_____

_____

As the grasshopper-sized spies demonstrated, fear can really mess up your sense of proportion. Think of the biggest challenges or problems you face right now. Is fear causing you to exaggerate their size? Is fear causing you to shrink in your own estimation?

_____

_____

_____

Genuine Wisdom, Genuine Love

> *Then the woman whose child was the living one spoke to the king, for she was deeply stirred over her son and said, "Oh, my lord, give her the living child, and by no means kill him." But the other said, "He shall be neither mine nor yours; divide him!"*
>
> 1 Kings 3:26 NASB

The Big Picture

It was a terrible dilemma. Two women came before King Solomon to settle a question of child custody. The women shared a house, and both of them had babies who were born only three days apart. In the middle of the night, one of the mothers accidentally rolled over on her baby and smothered it. Thus far the women agreed on the facts of the matter. The problem was that each woman claimed that the surviving baby belonged to her. The one woman said that the other woman had swapped babies in the middle of the night. The second woman said no, the first woman had made up the whole baby-swapping story after she woke up and realized she had smothered her own baby.

It was just one woman's word against another's. There were no witnesses in the house the night all this happened. Neither woman was married, so there were no husbands to confirm the baby's identity. The baby wasn't old enough to say for himself who his mother was. And apparently nobody else knew the baby well enough to say which woman it belonged to. The case

take a **CLOSER** look for teens

must have worked its way up from a local magistrate and through one or more appellate courts—who knows how many levels—before it was brought before King Solomon.

The usual legal proceedings were obviously of no use. So Solomon came up with a most unusual legal procedure. He called for a sword. Since things were obviously at a deadlock, he said, there was nothing to do but cut the baby in two and give a half to each mother. One woman turned pale. But only one. She said, "Oh, my lord, give her the living child, and by no means kill him." But the other woman said, "He shall be neither mine nor yours; divide him!"

Solomon, of course, knew immediately which woman the boy belonged to. What mother would allow her child to be cut in half? Of course the woman who willingly gave up the child was the real mother. You wonder if Solomon had seen something in the women's faces—some glint of envy in the false mother's eye, perhaps—that tipped him off, that told him his gamble would work. In any case, Solomon obviously understood human beings inside and out. He proved that his reputation for wisdom was well deserved.

You can't access wisdom by the megabyte.
Wisdom is concerned with how we relate to
people, to the world, and to God.

Edmund P. Clowney

The story of Solomon offering to divide the child is often told to illustrate the wisdom of Solomon. But it also illustrates something very important about the nature of real love. Sometimes loving another person means keeping a loose grip on him or her. Sometimes a person says he loves another person when what he really means is that he would like to possess that person. But real love is about seeking what is best for someone else, and not using him or her for self-gratification.

When the two women first came before Solomon, love was indistinguishable from mere possessiveness. A woman who truly loved a baby and a woman who merely wanted to possess it would do the same thing in that situation: she would fight to maintain custody. Solomon's genius was creating a situation where love and possessiveness would not react in the same way. For a person motivated by possessiveness—and worse, by envy—half a baby is better than no baby. For a person motivated by love, half a baby is much worse than no baby. By forcing the issue, Solomon made the difference obvious.

> *Love suffers long and is kind; love does not envy . . . does not seek its own.*
>
> 1 Corinthians 13:4–5 NKJV

There are a lot of things that can masquerade as love—infatuation, lust, insecurity, the desire to possess. If somebody says he or she loves you, it's worth asking the question "What does this person mean by 'love'?" Jesus defined love as the willingness to lay down your life for a friend. To put it another way, it's a willingness to put another person's interests ahead of your own interests. It's a refusal to use another person for your own purposes. Do the people who claim to love you really love like that?

How about you? How well do you love other people? If you love only the lovable, it's possible you're mistaking love for a simple reaction to another person's lovableness. You get pleasure from being around lovable people. That's fine, but you need to realize you're still thinking about you and your desires. How willing are you to put that person's interests ahead of your own? When there's nothing in it for you, how willingly would you go out of your way to see that person happy and fulfilled? If it came to it, how willingly would you let go, like the mother who stood before Solomon?

In real love you want the other person's good. In romantic love, you want the other person.

Margaret Anderson

Helen Keller was an inspiration to the world with her bravery and perseverance in spite of being both blind and deaf. Keller was inspired by the love of her teacher, Anne Sullivan. She recalls the day Miss Sullivan explained the meaning of the word *love*:

"'What is love?' I asked. . . . 'Love is something like the clouds that were in the sky before the sun came out,' she replied. . . . 'You cannot touch the clouds, you know; but you feel the rain and know how glad the flowers and the thirsty earth are to have it after a hot day. You cannot touch love either; but you feel the sweetness that it pours into everything. Without love you would not be happy or want to play.'

"The beautiful truth burst upon my mind—I felt that these were invisible lines stretched between my spirit and the spirits of others."

Zooming **In**

Wouldn't there have been somebody who knew the baby well enough to testify to its identity? Not necessarily. According to Jewish law, a woman was ceremonially unclean for forty days after childbirth and would be more or less confined to the house. Since the two women were prostitutes, they probably didn't have family coming to visit at the house.

The Bible states that Solomon was the wisest of rulers, and Solomon left the biblical books of Proverbs, the Song of Solomon, and Ecclesiastes as evidence of his wisdom. But the story of Solomon and the two mothers is really the only example in Scripture of Solomon's wisdom in action.

It takes a wise person to know the difference between real love and its counterfeits. But the good news is that you don't have to be as wise as Solomon to know the difference. Spend some time reflecting on your own attitudes toward love—and your behavior toward your loved ones.

List five people you love—some family members, some not family members. How does your love for those people stack up against Jesus' definition of love? How willing are you to lay down your life for them, to put their interests ahead of your own?

_____

_____

_____

Read 1 Corinthians 13, preferably in a translation you're not already familiar with. Think about that list of characteristics of genuine love. Which ones are the hardest for you? Which come most naturally?

_____

_____

_____

Solomon received wisdom before he asked for it. That's God's promise: anyone who sincerely asks for wisdom will receive it. Write out a prayer for wisdom in some area of your life where you especially need it.

_____

_____

_____

Servant Leader

Stephen, full of grace and power, was performing great wonders and signs among the people.

But some men . . . rose up and argued with Stephen.

But they were unable to cope with the wisdom and the Spirit with which he was speaking.

Acts 6:8–10 NASB

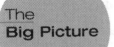

The
Big Picture

Stephen was famous for being the first follower of Jesus to die for his faith. An angry mob, led by the Pharisees, stoned him to death outside Jerusalem. Besides being the first martyr, Stephen was also the first deacon. The original job of deacons, believe it or not, was food service. The early Christians ate meals together every day—or at least they served meals to the poorer church members every day. As the church grew, this became a bigger and bigger task, and it became increasingly difficult to distribute the food fairly. The Gentile Christians—those who came to the church from non-Jewish backgrounds—came to believe that their widows were being overlooked in favor of the Jewish widows. This issue had the potential to become divisive. The disciples had been preaching that Jesus died not only for the Jews, but also for the Gentiles. But now, when the rubber met the road, they appeared to be treating the Gentiles like second-class citizens.

The twelve apostles recognized the problem. The last thing they wanted was to give the impression that the Gentile widows were less valuable in

God's eyes than the Jewish widows. But they were swamped. They were preaching constantly and dealing with hostile religious leaders and trying to figure out how to "do" church. They simply didn't have time to oversee the distribution of food and ensure it was done fairly. Even if they straightened out this one conflict, more would inevitably arise, and they just couldn't deal with it on a daily basis and still devote themselves to God's Word.

So they decided to delegate the responsibility. They had the congregation select seven men to be responsible for the serving of meals. The first man chosen was Stephen. He was a good choice, for not only was he a natural leader and "full of faith and of the Holy Spirit" (Acts 6:5 NASB), he was also a Gentile himself.

Stephen humbly took on the role of food-service worker so that the gospel of Jesus could go forward. By taking care of the widows of the church—and by making sure the Gentiles were treated as the equals of the Jews—Stephen gave hands and feet to the gospel that was being preached by the apostles.

God has called us to shine. Let no one say he cannot shine because he has not so much influence as some others may have. What God wants you to do is to use the influence you have.

Dwight L. Moody

For Stephen, serving meals and preaching the gospel went hand in hand. Being assigned a support role didn't let him off the hook for being a witness. If anything, it increased his sense of responsibility. Sure, his official job was waiting tables, but he still performed signs and wonders, and he still boldly preached the Word of God. It's ironic: the whole reason Stephen took responsibility for the meals was so that the apostles could devote more time to their preaching; but it was Stephen, not any of the apostles, whose preaching first angered the religious leaders to the point of murder.

Just as Stephen's food-service ministry was focused on reaching out to the Gentiles with God's love, his preaching was also focused on God's love for the Gentiles. That's what made the Pharisees so mad. They didn't appreciate it one bit when this Gentile Stephen stood up to declare that God loved Gentiles as much as he loved the Jews. Stephen might have buried himself in the work of serving meals. It was important work, after all. But he didn't. And because he was willing to speak boldly on the streets of Jerusalem, his influence has echoed through two thousand years.

Always be ready to give a defense to anyone who asks you a reason for the hope that is in you.

1 Peter 3:15 HCSB

You don't have to be a preacher to serve God. People have different talents and abilities, different temperaments and interests. You can sing in the choir or keep the nursery or paint a Sunday school room. Beyond the church walls, you can get involved in tutoring or mentoring or some other community volunteer service. You're communicating the gospel when you do those things; you're demonstrating the love of God by putting other people's interests ahead of your own.

Apply It to Your Life

But bear this in mind; just because you find a way to communicate the love of God in a support role, that doesn't necessarily mean you're exempt from actually speaking the gospel. The Bible says you should always be ready to give an account of the hope that is within you. You may be tempted to say, "I do my bit. I ladle up soup at the soup kitchen; I leave the preaching to someone else." As Stephen's life shows, it's all one thing. The same truths that motivate your actions should motivate your speech. The service you do with your hands and feet doesn't exempt you from speaking on behalf of Jesus. Rather, it should give you opportunity to speak.

It is the duty of every Christian to be Christ to his neighbor.
Martin Luther

Missionary Amy Carmichael served in India, where she met many, many physical needs. She was a servant leader. Here are some of her thoughts on what it means to love and to lead:

"If I am afraid to speak the truth, lest I lose affection, or lest the one concerned should say, 'You do not understand,' or because I fear to lose my reputation for kindness; if I put my own good name before the other's highest good, then I know nothing of Calvary love. If I myself dominate myself, if my thoughts revolve around myself, if I am so occupied with myself I rarely have 'a heart at leisure from itself,' then I know nothing of Calvary love. If I cannot in honest happiness take the second place (or twentieth); if I cannot take the first without making a fuss about my unworthiness, then I know nothing of Calvary love. If I do not give a friend 'the benefit of the doubt,' but put the worst construction instead of the best on what is said or done, then I know nothing of Calvary love."

Zooming In

Though the seven men chosen to relieve the apostles of their food-service duties are recognized as the first deacons, they aren't actually called deacons in Acts. That title (for the same office) comes later. The Greek word for deacon, *diakanos,* literally means "servant." It is used elsewhere to describe household servants and personal attendants.

After Stephen was killed, his fellow deacon, Philip, took his place. Like Stephen, Philip was a Gentile. Like Stephen, Philip carried the gospel out to the Gentile world. He lived much longer than Stephen, however. On Paul's last missionary journey, he visited Philip at home in Caesarea, where he had four daughters, all prophetesses.

The work of the gospel requires that people perform a lot of different tasks—from preaching to waiting tables. It's all one message: the love of God in action. How do you fit in?

Through the **Eyes of** Your Heart

Do you perform a support role in your church or in any other ministries? If not, why not? And if you are involved in that way, what are your motivations? Would you say you serve for the same reason preachers preach? Do you see your role as being part of the spread of the gospel?

What do you think: can a Christian be exempt from speaking the gospel? Why or why not?

If someone were to ask you to "give an answer . . . for the hope that you have" (1 Peter 3:15 NIV) what would you say?

Standing Firm

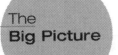

The **Big Picture**

A huge fire blazed in the city of Rome in July of AD 64. It started in the east-side slums and swept westward to engulf half the city. Even the palace of the emperor Nero was destroyed. Many Romans suspected that Nero himself started the fire. He was a lunatic, after all, and a particularly evil one at that. Perhaps he burned the city so he would have an excuse for rebuilding it on a grander scale. (He built some magnificent structures, including a new, 120-acre palace complex known as the Golden House.)

Whether Nero actually started the fire or not, it turned into a major political crisis for the emperor. He had to figure out some way to divert the blame away from himself. He decided to blame the whole thing on the fast-growing religious sect known as the Christians. It wasn't that hard to pin the crime on them. Their loyalty to Rome was questionable: they claimed that their true loyalty was not to Rome, but to God. They refused to worship the emperor. Besides, they were just different from everybody else. They didn't seem to share Roman values. Nero managed to convince himself and others that the

Christians were enemies of the state, just the sort of people who would set fire to the capital city.

The persecutions that followed were horrible. Christians were arrested and killed en masse. They were burned at the stake and fed to the lions for the entertainment of cheering crowds. They were used as victims in bloody gladiator games.

This was the environment in which Peter sat down to write the letter now known as the New Testament book of 1 Peter. He lived in the city of Rome, and he knew the persecutions would soon be spreading throughout the empire, if they hadn't already. He wrote his letter to be circulated among the churches in Asia Minor, modern-day Turkey. It was a letter of hope and encouragement in the midst of serious danger: things are tough all over, Peter said, but God is good. Even if the tide of persecution was irresistible, even if suffering was inevitable, that didn't mean the church would crumble. Yes, the devil was on the prowl. But the Christians in Asia Minor—and all over the world—could resist him.

You don't live in a world all alone.
Your brothers are here too.
Albert Schweitzer

Suffering feels like a very personal thing. When you're the one tied to the stake, it feels very much like your problem. But take a closer look at what Peter is saying in this passage. There is definitely a communal component to suffering. Peter reminded his brothers and sisters in Asia Minor that they were all in it together. The way they conducted themselves under persecution would affect not just themselves, not just their neighbors, but believers all over the world.

Peter told his readers to resist the devil, knowing that the same sufferings were being experienced by their brothers and sisters everywhere. Christianity had spread throughout the Roman Empire, and believers throughout that vast area were all in the same boat. The verse in 1 Peter applies to you, as well. Everyone has similar experiences with the tough things in life. According to Peter, you know you *can* resist the devil because you can see that other believers have resisted. And you know you *must* resist the devil for the sake of others who look up to you. People derive strength from the strength of others. And their strength collapses when they see someone in the same situation giving up. Whether you decide to resist or surrender, Peter is saying, the effects of your choice ripple out in every direction.

> *Resist the devil, and he will flee from you.*
>
> James 4:7 NIV

The devil is still prowling and seeking to destroy those who belong to Jesus. In some parts of the world, he's still using the tactics he used in the Roman Empire: terror, torture, death. But historically that hasn't been a very good way of stopping the church. As believers stand firm under that kind of persecution, the church only gets stronger. In

Apply It
to Your Life

this country, Satan's tactics tend to be subtler. Believers affirm or deny their faith not at the point of an executioner's sword, but in daily choices: will you conform to the materialism and self-indulgence of the world around you? Will you allow yourself and your faith to become totally irrelevant to a dying world?

Every hour of every day you have a choice: to compromise and conform, or to help in the transformation of this culture. The choice you make will affect your life greatly. But it won't just affect you. As other believers see you taking a stand, they will be strengthened to take a stand, and who knows how far the effects will ripple out? If you choose to cave, it makes it that much easier for the next guy to cave.

We cannot live only for ourselves. A thousand fibers connect us with our fellow men!

Herman Melville

It has been said that the blood of the martyrs is the seed of the church. Here's what Martin Luther had to say on the subject:

"If the devil were wise enough and would stand by in silence and let the gospel be preached, he would suffer less harm. For when there is no battle for the gospel . . . it finds no cause and no occasion to show its vigor and power. Therefore, nothing better can befall the gospel than that the world should fight it."

Walter Hilton recalls Jesus' warning to his disciples that all who follow after him would experience persecution:

"When your enemies see that you are so determined that neither sickness, fancies, poverty, life, death, nor sins discourage you, but that you will continue to seek the love of Jesus and nothing else, by continuing your prayer and other spiritual works, they will grow enraged and will not spare you the most cruel abuse."

Zooming In

In his *Annals*, the Roman historian Tacitus describes Nero's persecution of the Christians after the great fire in Rome. According to Tacitus, Christians were sewn into the hides of animals and torn to bits by dogs; they were crucified; they were set on fire to be used as lamps at night. Tacitus himself hated Christians. He called Christianity a "destructive superstition" and said Christians were clearly guilty (though not guilty of setting the fire) and deserved to be punished. But he hated Nero even more. He regretted that Nero's cruelty caused people to have pity on the Christians.

Jesus made it clear that Christians who are serious about following after him will experience persecution. That being the case, it's important that Christians be ready and willing to support one another and set a good example for one another. You aren't an island; your choices affect your fellow believers.

Would you say that Christians experience persecution at your school or in any of your other social settings? If so, what form does it take? If not, why do you think that is?

_____

_____

_____

Write about a time when you were encouraged by another Christian's commitment to stand firm.

_____

_____

_____

_____

Have you ever experienced discouragement because of a fellow believer's failure to stand firm? If so, write about it.

_____

_____

_____

_____

Where's the Temple?

I saw no temple in [the New Jerusalem], for the Lord God the Almighty and the Lamb are its temple.

Revelation 21:22 NASB

The Big Picture

The emperor Domitian exiled the apostle John to the island of Patmos, in the Grecian archipelago. Actually, to call it an island is almost to give Patmos too much credit; it was more like a big rock jutting out of the Aegean Sea, where a very old man was sent to live out the end of his days so he wouldn't cause any more trouble for the powers that be. Against that barren and empty backdrop, John had the incredible vision that he wrote down as the book of Revelation. Living on earth at its bleakest, John got a glimpse of heaven in its glory.

The new heaven and the new earth—John saw all the effects of the Fall reversed. The sin of Adam and Eve introduced all the unhappiness and difficulty that we now call "just the way it is": sickness, sadness, pain, death, disappointment, brokenness. God gave John a look at a place where all that was gone, where things worked the way they would have worked all along if sin hadn't spoiled everything. In this vision, God will dwell among his people, "and He will wipe away every tear from their eyes; and there will no longer be any death; there will no longer be any mourning, or crying, or pain; the first things have passed away" (Revelation 21:4 NASB). All things will be made new.

In his vision, John saw a beautiful city—the New Jerusalem. Again, it is a place where everything is the way it should have been all along. God is there, so there is no need for a sun or moon to light the place. God's glory provides brilliant light, so it is daytime all the time. Beautiful, jewel-encrusted walls form perfect square walls for the city's boundaries. There are twelve gates in the walls, each carved from a single huge pearl. But the gates are always open; there are no enemies to shut them against.

John saw all the nations walking in the light of God's glory. In its perfected state, the New Jerusalem isn't a place for just one nation or ethnic group. It's a place where all nations bring the best of their culture as an offering to God. All the truly good things about earth will survive in the new heaven and new earth, and all the bad things will fly away, forgotten.

My heaven is to please God and glorify him, and to give all to him, and to be wholly devoted to his glory; that is the heaven I long for.

David Brainerd

The New Jerusalem didn't have a temple in John's vision. Throughout history, the temple had always been one of the key features of the old Jerusalem. Solomon's temple was the glory of Israel until it was destroyed by the Babylonian king Nebuchadnezzar in 586 BC. When the Jews returned from exile fifty years later, they went right to work building a second, much-less-grand temple. That temple was replaced by a magnificent one built by the Herods around the time of Jesus. But that temple was totally destroyed by the Romans in AD 70, only seven or eight years after its completion.

The people of Jerusalem mourned the loss of their beautiful temples. So you would expect the new, perfected Jerusalem to have an unimaginably magnificent temple. But that's not the case. In the presence of God, there's no need for a temple. When the glories of God are visible already, what architectural marvel could further reveal his glory? John's vision of the New Jerusalem shows that all earthly reminders of God are really just a means to an end. Hopefully, they point you toward God. But there's no need to get too attached to them. God's presence is the real goal.

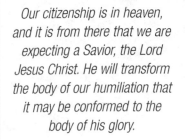

Our citizenship is in heaven, and it is from there that we are expecting a Savior, the Lord Jesus Christ. He will transform the body of our humiliation that it may be conformed to the body of his glory.

Philippians 3:20–21 NRSV

God's idea of a perfect world is a world without churches. Or, to put it more precisely, a perfect world wouldn't *need* churches. Unfortunately, this isn't a perfect world. So we need churches very much. Because you can't see God in his full glory, you need a place where you can block out the concerns of daily life and focus on what ultimately matters. You need other believers to encourage you in your walk, and you need to encourage other believers. You need some set-aside time to worship and sing praises to God.

Apply It to Your Life

You haven't gotten to the new heaven and new earth yet, so church is something you need to take seriously. Just don't take it more seriously than you take God. If you're active in a church, you know how quickly youth group and other activities can fill up your life. That's a good thing—certainly better than a lot of things that could fill up your life. Just remember that church is a means to an end. The real point is to pursue God. Is your church experience truly pointing you toward a deeper walk with God? If not, you might want to rethink the way you do church.

A continual looking forward to the eternal world is not a form of escapism or wishful thinking, but one of the things a Christian is meant to do.

C. S. Lewis

As Jonathan Edwards said, the enjoyment of God is the only happiness that satisfies the soul. That enjoyment can be complete only in heaven.

"To go to heaven, fully to enjoy God, is infinitely better than the most pleasant accommodations here. Fathers and mothers, wives, or children, or the company of earthly friends, are but the shadows; but God is the substance. They are scattered beams, but God is the sun. These are but streams. But God is the ocean."

John Stott offers this beautiful picture of what believers have to look forward to when they get to heaven:

"The King of the universe will grant us refuge in the shelter of his throne, where we may see him and worship him day and night in his temple, and the Lamb turned Shepherd will lead us with the rest of his sheep to fountains of living water, where we may slake our thirst forever at the eternal springs."

Zooming In

Biblical scholars say that John's Greek grammar in the book of Revelation is rough. Unlike Paul and Luke, the apostle John wasn't well educated. So why weren't his Gospel and his three epistles just as rough? John probably wrote those books in Ephesus, surrounded by friends who could review his writing before he sent it out. In Patmos he was all alone. Then there's the fact that John was probably in a state of great excitement when he wrote the Revelation, having just seen what was surely the most incredible vision ever recorded. It would have been hard to write at all, much less write with perfect grammar!

Through the Eyes of Your Heart

In the perfect city in John's vision, there was no temple, no place of worship. How do you explain this surprising fact?

_____

_____

_____

_____

Just because there's no temple or church in the new earth, does that mean we'd be better off without church on this earth? Why or why not?

_____

_____

_____

_____

How would you describe your church experience? Does going to church do for you what it's supposed to do? How does Sunday morning worship put you on the road toward a deeper relationship with God? What would you change?

_____

_____

_____

Thankful Heart, Peaceful Heart

Do not be anxious about anything, but in everything, by prayer and petition, with thanksgiving, present your requests to God. And the peace of God, which transcends all understanding, will guard your hearts and your minds in Christ Jesus.

Philippians 4:6–7 NIV

The Big Picture

The Philippian church had a special place in the apostle Paul's heart. When he began his missionary work, the Philippians were the first church to give him the financial support he needed to keep going. Years later, when Paul found himself imprisoned in Rome, the Philippians came through again. They took up a collection and sent one of their members, a man named Epaphroditus, to deliver the gift to Paul in prison.

The New Testament book of Philippians is Paul's thank-you note for the Philippians' gift. Epaphroditus hand-delivered the letter when he went home to Philippi. Paul's joy is bursting out all over the place in this letter—which is ironic, when you consider the fact that he was in jail when he wrote it, waiting for a trial that could easily end in a death sentence. No doubt Paul was cheered by the presence of his old friend Epaphroditus. But there was more to it than that. In prison Paul had realized that following Christ meant having nothing to lose and everything to gain. "For to me, to live is Christ and to die is gain" (Philippians 1:21 NIV), he wrote. If the Roman government lets him live, awesome! If the Roman government puts him to death, even better! He gets to go home to heaven. It's hard to defeat a person with an attitude like that.

Paul already knew that God's purposes could never be thwarted, not even by the Roman Empire. But it had to have been a huge rush to see that truth in action. The Romans had imprisoned him in order to slow the spread of the gospel. But through Paul's contact with the prison guards, God had already made converts in the famed Praetorian Guard and even within Caesar's household.

So Paul wasn't just talking when he told his friends in Philippi, "Do not be anxious about anything." If anybody's earthly situation ever gave him reason to be anxious, surely it was Paul's in a Roman prison. He was on the wrong side of the most powerful empire the world had ever seen. They could squash him like a bug. But Paul found peace. While his body was being guarded by the Praetorian Guard, his heart was being guarded by "the peace of God, which transcends all understanding."

When there is a storm without, [God] will make peace within. The world can create trouble in peace, but God can create peace in trouble.

Thomas Watson

You may not spend a lot of time examining the verbal structure of Scripture passages. But in the case of Philippians 4:6–7, it may be worth your time. Think of this passage as a sandwich. In the center are the words, "with thanksgiving." On either side of thanksgiving is prayer. Immediately before the words "with thanksgiving," you see the words "by prayer and petition." Immediately after, you see the words "present your requests to God"—which is just another way of saying "prayer and petition." Thanksgiving is the meat between two slices of prayer. Look again at the passage: it's actually a double-decker sandwich. On either side of prayer, you have two slices of peace: "Do not be anxious . . ." and "the peace of God . . ."

Peace, wrapped around prayer, wrapped around thanksgiving. The structure of this passage is a clue to Paul's meaning. Everybody wants peace. What's at the center of peace? Prayer. What's at the center of prayer? Thanksgiving. That's how things worked out for Paul. God had done incredible things in Paul's life, and it made him thankful. That thankfulness motivated him to keep praying. And a rich prayer life led to the peace—and joy—that shines so clearly in the book of Philippians.

In everything give thanks; for this is the will of God in Christ Jesus for you.

1 Thessalonians 5:18 NKJV

There are certain things in life that you don't get by going after them directly. You don't get respect, for example, by demanding that everyone respect you. You get respect by keeping your promises, trying your hardest, fulfilling your responsibilities—somewhere along the line you realize that people respect you. Peace is the same way. You can't just declare, "I'm going to feel peaceful. I'm going to feel peaceful. I'm going to feel peaceful." You can work yourself into a frenzy trying to work up a feeling of peace.

Apply It to Your Life

As Paul's experience shows, the peace of God comes from an abiding trust in God. That kind of trust comes from seeing your prayers answered. And an active prayer life is fueled by a spirit of thanksgiving. As you reflect on the ways God has been good to you, you're motivated to keep praying. As God answers prayer, you feel greater peace *and* greater thankfulness. It's a beautiful cycle.

There's a lot in your life to stress you out—exams, relationships, parents who don't seem to understand you. It's not always easy to find peace. As it turns out, you find peace by looking in an unexpected place: in thankfulness.

We are not at peace with others because we are not at peace with ourselves, and we are not at peace with ourselves because we are not at peace with God.

Thomas Merton

Jonathan Aitken was a member of the British Parliament who was imprisoned for perjury. Like the apostle Paul, he experienced peace in an unexpected place:

"I was in Chelsea police station where I was charged with perjury and conspiracy to pervert public justice. I spent the next five hours alone in a police cell while waiting for the various formalities such as fingerprinting and photographs. I used that time to pray, to meditate and to read all sixteen chapters of St. Mark's Gospel. . . . I had such an overwhelming sense of God's presence in the cell with me that I was at peace."

A. W. Tozer draws a connection between peace and the ability to forget about yourself. Peace comes when you are free from self-worship:

"The labor of self-love is a heavy one indeed. Think for yourself whether much of your sorrow has not arisen from someone speaking slightingly of you. As long as you set yourself up as a little god to which you must be loyal, how can you hope to find inward peace?"

Zooming **In**

Philippians is surely one of the most joyful books ever written. How much joy is there in this book? The words *joy* and *rejoice* appear nineteen times in just 104 verses—a mention of joy every 5.1 verses. That's a whole lot of joy for a guy who's locked in a Roman prison!

It is believed that Paul wrote at least four books of the Bible while he was in prison: Colossians, Philemon, Ephesians, and Philippians. Paul rejoiced in Philippians that the gospel was spreading in spite of his imprisonment. He had no idea how true that would be. Think how much the gospel has spread as a result of those four books he wrote in prison.

"Blessed are the peacemakers" (Matthew 5:9 NKJV). Everybody wants a life of peace. Paul's route seems indirect, but you can be confident it will get you there: thankfulness produces an active prayer life, and an active prayer life produces peace.

How do you define peace? What would peace look like in your life?

_____

_____

_____

_____

You've heard the saying "Count your blessings." It's actually not a bad idea. Start a list of things you have to be thankful for.

_____

_____

_____

_____

As long as you are making lists, make a list of things you're praying about. Leave a column for writing a date for when each prayer is answered. Not only will such a list help you remember what to pray for, it will deliver encouragement and peace when you look back and see how God has been faithful.

_____

_____

_____

Clean Heart, Confident Heart

> *Beloved, if our heart does not condemn us, we have confidence before God; and whatever we ask we receive from Him, because we keep His commandments and do the things that are pleasing in His sight.*
>
> 1 John 3:21–22 NASB

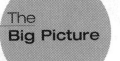

The Big Picture

The apostle John referred to himself in his Gospel as "the disciple whom Jesus loved." Indeed, he did seem to have an especially close and loving relationship with Jesus. When Jesus was dying on the cross, John was the person to whom he gave the task of looking after his mother Mary. Perhaps it shouldn't be surprising, then, that in his letters John was fascinated with the idea of love—specifically, how love gives shape to a life that pleases God.

The book of 1 John in particular explores the relationship between love and obedience. "This is the love of God," wrote John, "that we keep His commandments" (1 John 5:3 NASB). The legalist in us nods in agreement. The natural impulse of the Pharisee is to believe that you love God more by taking on greater burdens and making more sacrifices for his sake. John turns that upside down: "His commandments are not burdensome" (5:3 NASB). They aren't burdensome because loving God means desiring what God desires. For those who truly love God, obedience becomes more and more natural.

Sometimes, of course, obedience is hard; sometimes it truly is a matter of sacrificing your will to God's will. But as you love God more and more, the equation begins to change.

Love is the key to right living. Love your neighbor, and you do right by your neighbor. Love God, and you obey his commands. Your conscience is clean. Your heart doesn't condemn you. And as John says, "If our heart does not condemn us, we have confidence before God." He goes on to say that when we have that confidence before God, we receive whatever we ask of God because we please him. It's a big, beautiful cycle: When you love God, you find it easier to obey God. When you obey God, your heart doesn't condemn you. When your heart doesn't condemn you, you pray freely and see the fruit of those prayers. When God answers your prayers, your confidence in God grows and you love him more deeply. Which makes it even easier to be obedient. Part of the Christian life is becoming more and more sensitive to your own sins and shortcomings. How, then, are you supposed to have a clear conscience? By having more and more confidence in the God who delights to cleanse you of your sin.

Most of us follow our conscience as we follow a wheelbarrow. We push it in front of us in the direction we want to go.

Billy Graham

"If our heart does not condemn us, we have confidence before God." If you're not careful here, you can get the impression that John is saying, "As long as your conscience doesn't bother you, you and God are cool." But there are lots of people who have "clear consciences" without pleasing God. Consider self-righteous people who think they're always right and everybody else is wrong. Their consciences feel pretty good most of the time, but they aren't living a life that pleases God. Or what about people who don't even care what's right and what's wrong? Their hearts aren't condemning them. But that doesn't mean they can come before God with confidence.

John's idea of having a heart that doesn't condemn you all comes down to the idea of love. As you love God, you love your neighbor and you develop the right habits. You desire what's right; your heart has less to condemn you for. And here's the key: as you experience God's love more fully, you are free from the condemnation you feel when you do slip up. You might say your confidence before God results in a clear conscience, not the other way around.

> *Create in me a clean heart,
> O God, and renew a steadfast
> spirit within me.*
>
> Psalm 51:10 NKJV

Do you find it hard to keep your conscience clear? Do you struggle with guilt and condemnation? There is hope for you. First, take heart in the fact that your heart is soft. God doesn't do a lot of work in the heart of a person who is too self-confident to need God. Nor does he do a lot of work in the heart that is too hard to feel guilt. That gnawing conscience is a sign that you've got a heart God can work with.

Apply It to Your Life

Second, you need to get yourself free from the idea that you need to work a little harder, sacrifice a little more, shoulder a heavier burden in order to clear your conscience and get right with God. There is no path leading from good works to the love of God. It's a one-way path, and it goes in the opposite direction. Start with the love of God, and good works will follow as a natural result—not merely good works, but the kind of good works that actually please God. That kind of life fills you with genuine confidence in the God who is faithful even when you are faithless.

Peace of conscience is nothing but the echo of pardoning mercy.

William Gurnall

Richard P. McBrien understood what the apostle John was saying about love. A clear conscience, right living, and our confidence before God all begin with love:

"Love is closely related to the will. Will without love becomes manipulation; love without will becomes sentimentality. We are afraid, in the latter case, that if we choose one person rather than another, we will lose something, and we are too insecure to take that chance. . . . If love is the soul of Christian existence, it must be at the heart of every other Christian virtue. Thus, for example, justice without love is legalism; faith without love is ideology; hope without love is self-centeredness; forgiveness without love is self-abasement; fortitude without love is recklessness; generosity without love is extravagance; care without love is mere duty; fidelity without love is servitude. Every virtue is an expression of love. No virtue is really a virtue unless it is permeated, or informed, by love."

Zooming **In**

When John says that we have "confidence" before God, he is using the Greek word *parresia*. *Parresia* is a pretty common word in the New Testament, and it means freedom or unreservedness in speech. One of the definitions in Vine's dictionary is "cheerful courage." In the book of Acts, the disciples are often described as displaying *parresia* as they boldly proclaim the gospel to people who were hostile to their message. If your heart does not condemn you, you need not cringe and cower before God's throne. A clear conscience gives you boldness—a "cheerful courage"—as you speak to God.

David longed for a clean heart. Jesus promised that the pure in heart would be blessed, "for they shall see God." But you're been around long enough to know that it's no easy matter for a human being to keep a clean heart.

How is the rest of your life affected when your heart condemns you? How are things different when your conscience is clear?

_____

_____

_____

_____

What are some things that you need to get off your conscience? How do you do that?

_____

_____

_____

_____

How do you need to love people differently in order to live a life that's more pleasing to God?

_____

_____

_____

_____

Lukewarm

The Big Picture

The book of Revelation begins with specific messages or "letters" to seven churches in Asia Minor, in modern-day Turkey. Each of these churches had its own personality, as well as its own particular challenges and its own weaknesses. The church at Ephesus had worked hard and persevered in spite of hardship. But they weren't a very loving church, and Jesus corrected them for that. The church at Smyrna was poor and suffered persecution. To them, Jesus offered words of hope. Pergamos had its good points, but it tolerated false teachings among some of its members. The church at Thyatira had done good things, too, but was struggling with immorality. Sardis looked good on the outside and had a good reputation, but Jesus accused them of being dead. The church at Philadelphia, on the other hand, was a faithful church, and Jesus promised them victory.

The seventh and final church on the list was the church at Laodicea. This was the only church about which Jesus had nothing good to say. He didn't mention any "big" sins, like the heresy at Pergamos or the sexual immorality at Thyatira. The Laodiceans' problem was less spectacular but more insidious. They simply had no passion for God. "I know your works," said Jesus, "that you are neither cold nor hot. So then, because you are lukewarm, . . . I will vomit you out of My mouth." Hot coffee or tea is great; iced tea or coffee is very refreshing; but lukewarm, room-temperature coffee or tea isn't fit to drink. You want to spit it back out when you get a mouthful. In the same way, Jesus said, the lukewarm, dispassionate attitude of the Laodicean Christians made him want to vomit.

The church at Laodicea could look at itself and think it was doing pretty well. No "major" sins were damaging their reputation or pricking their consciences. They apparently weren't suffering any persecutions. But perhaps that was their problem. They had nothing to be passionate about, good or bad. Open sin is something God can deal with. A burning passion (even if it is sometimes misdirected) is something God can work with. But lukewarm, self-satisfied churchgoers just going through the motions make God want to puke.

I prefer a sinful man who knows he has sinned and repents, to a man who has not sinned and considers himself to be righteous.

Abba Samartas

The Laodiceans' biggest problem was the fact that they were satisfied with themselves the way they were. They were lukewarm toward Jesus because they didn't really feel they needed him. Jesus' message to the Laodiceans is a point-by-point rebuttal of everything they took pride in. "You say, 'I am rich, and have become wealthy, and have need of nothing'" (Revelation 3:17 NASB). In earthly terms, they really didn't need much. Laodicea was a famously wealthy city. When an earthquake destroyed several towns and cities in the region, Laodicea was the only city that refused aid from the Roman government. They had plenty of wealth to rebuild on their own terms.

The Laodiceans "had need of nothing." But Jesus said they were "poor and blind and naked" (Revelation 3:17 NASB). He was hitting on three points of civic pride. Laodicea was an important banking center. But Jesus said they were poor. Laodicea also had a reputation for producing medicinal powders to treat eye ailments. But Jesus said they were blind. Third, Laodicea was famous for producing garments of a fine black wool. But Jesus said they were naked. He invited the Laodiceans to come to him for true riches, for true salve to heal their blindness, and for white garments to cover their nakedness. But as long as the Laodiceans trusted in their own resources, it would never happen.

> *If riches increase, do not set your heart on them.*
>
> Psalm 62:10 NKJV

It's hard to get passionate about God when you feel you have everything under control. The promises of God cut both ways. You're never too sinful to receive God's forgiveness. You're never too poor to receive God's riches. You're never too sick to receive God's healing. But as long as you feel that you're doing fine on your own, you're never going to be in a position to receive what he offers. You'll remain lukewarm. And lukewarm people make Jesus want to vomit.

Apply It to Your Life

What are you relying on? What are you drawing your strength from? It's painful when the things of earth fail you. When you fail the test you thought you were ready for. When that relationship breaks up—the one you thought would last forever. When you realize that credit card has enslaved you rather than setting you free. But those are the moments when you realize that you can't rely on the things of earth. You feel your lukewarmness for God begin to warm with the realization that you have nowhere else to turn. When you are no longer comfortable with the way things are, that's when you're in a place to see God work incredible changes in your life.

Complacency is the deadly foe of all spiritual growth.
A.W. Tozer

According to Horatius Bonar, godly dissatisfaction is a whole lot better than a complacency based on false confidence:

"'I am not satisfied with my faith,' says one. No, of course you aren't; nor will you ever be, at least I hope not! If you wait for this before you take peace, you will wait till life is done. It would appear that you want to believe in your own faith, in order to obtain rest to your soul. The Bible does not say, 'Being satisfied about our faith, we have peace with God,' but 'Being justified by faith, we have peace with God.' . . . 'I am not satisfied with my love.' What? Did you expect, on this earth, to be satisfied with any grace found in you? Was it your love for Christ or his love for you that gave you peace at first?

"Now then, there is but one thing with which Almighty God is entirely satisfied, and that is THE PERSON AND WORK OF HIS SON! It is with Christ that we must be satisfied, not with ourselves, nor anything about us!"

Zooming In

The one thing Laodicea didn't have was a good water supply. Colosse, a few miles in one direction, had a spring of cool, refreshing water. Hieropolis, a few miles in the other direction, had a hot spring famous for its healing properties. But Laodicea had neither cold water nor hot. Its water was brought in by aqueduct from a hot spring several miles away. By the time it got to the city, the mineral-heavy water was lukewarm and disgusting. So the Laodiceans would have known exactly what Jesus was talking about when he said their lukewarm attitude made him want to vomit.

Through the
Eyes of
Your Heart

Would you describe your passion for the things of God as hot, cold, or lukewarm? Why did you choose your answer?

_____

_____

_____

_____

What are areas of your life where you are in the most danger of becoming too comfortable?

_____

_____

_____

_____

What are the areas of your life where you need to let go of your discomfort and turn things over to God?

_____

_____

_____

_____

To Will, to Work

Work out your salvation with fear and trembling; for it is God who is at work in you, both to will and to work for His good pleasure.

Philippians 2:12–13 NASB

The Big Picture

The apostle Paul stood firm against anybody who would dare suggest that human beings could do anything to save themselves from their own sin. He had been rescued from that error himself, and he didn't want anybody else falling into it. Before he became a Christian, Paul was a Pharisee, one of the kings of self-righteousness. He knew all about working for God's approval, and he knew what a draining, ultimately ineffective way that was. All that self-righteousness of the Pharisees—everything he used to think was gain—he now counted it as rubbish—dung, actually (see Philippians 3:8). Throughout his missionary career, his great enemies were the Judaizers, who added extra rules and extra tasks to the simple message of God's grace through Christ.

Paul insisted that salvation came by grace alone. His letters breathe with God's grace: "By grace you have been saved" (Ephesians 2:5 NIV). "You know the grace of our Lord Jesus Christ, that though he was rich, yet for your sakes he became poor, so that you through his poverty might become rich"

take a **CLOSER** look for teens

(2 Corinthians 8:9 NIV). Why, then, would he write, "Work out your salvation with fear and trembling"? That sounds suspiciously similar to a works-based righteousness.

Paul says "work *out* your salvation," not "work *for* your salvation." And then he says why: "It is God who is at work in you, both to will and to work for his good pleasure." Once you've been saved, your desire is to please your Savior. And you do that by doing the work he has for you to do. In a way, it's not even your work; it's God's work that he does through you. Paul says something similar in Ephesians 2:8. It's one of the great grace passages of the Bible: "By grace you have been saved through faith; *and that not of yourselves*" (NASB, emphasis added). No works-righteousness there. But then, Paul declares that we are "created in Christ Jesus for good works, which God prepared beforehand, that we should walk in them" (Ephesians 2:10 ESV). The message is clear: good works can't save you; only God can do that. But once God has saved you, he's got work for you to do. Or, to put it another way, once he has saved you, it is God's good pleasure to do his work *through* you.

There are only two kinds of people in the end: those who say to God, "Thy will be done," and those to whom God says in the end, "Thy will be done."

C. S. Lewis

Paul said, "It is God who is at work in you." How does that work, exactly? It sounds sort of like God is making you do things, like you're some kind of zombie. But God doesn't zombify his followers. He works on your will, and in that way he influences you to do his work—"to will and to work for His good pleasure." That word *will* is all about desire. When God is at work in you, he helps you want the same things he wants. And when you want the same things God wants, you do the things that God wants done. The problem is that your old will is still hanging around, not yet ready to give up the fight. So there's always the possibility of wanting the wrong things—and therefore choosing to do the wrong things.

Notice what these verses don't say. They don't say anything about God's overruling anybody's ability to choose their actions. People always do as they please. It's a great mystery, this idea that God works through his people without overruling their ability to choose. But this tension appears throughout the Bible. God is at work . . . you'd better get to work!

> *Delight yourself in the LORD, and He will give you the desires of your heart.*
>
> Psalm 37:4 NASB

Martin Luther once said, "Love God, and do as you please." That's a good summary of how your free will relates to God's ability to work his will through you. Right actions begin with the right wants and desires. So why do you find yourself doing wrong even when you love God? Because you have conflicting desires. You love God, but your old self still loves self-indulgence. Sometimes that old self wins.

Apply It to Your Life

If you want to live a life of obedience, there's more to it than just trying harder. You're going to be more obedient when your desires are more in line with God's. Think about what you really want. Of course you have conflicting desires; everybody does. You want to make good grades, but there are a million things you'd rather do than study for those grades. You want to get up and have a quiet time in the morning, but you also want to sleep in. The question is, what do you want the *most*? If you're in Christ, you're going to realize that you want to please God more than you want all those things that don't please God. And that realization makes obedience a whole lot easier.

I find that doing the will of God leaves me with no time for disputing about his plans.

George Macdonald

Frances Ridley Havergal wrote the following as a bedtime devotion for children. But her interpretation of the phrase "to will and to work" is helpful to people of all ages:

"Have you not found it hard to be good? Hard to keep from saying something naughty that you wanted to say? Very hard to keep down the angry feeling, even if you did not say the angry word? Hard to do a right thing, because you did not at all like doing it, and quite impossible to make yourself wish to do it? You asked God to help you to do it, and he did help you; but did you ever think of asking him to make you like to do it?

"Now, this is just what is meant by God's 'working in you to will.' It means that he can and will undertake the very thing which you cannot manage. He can and will 'take your will, and work it for you'; making you want to do just what He wants you to do; making you like the very things that He likes, and hate just what He hates."

Zooming **In**

That word *will*—as in "to will and to work for his good pleasure"—is the Greek word *thelo,* meaning "desire" or "delight in." It applies equally to good desires and bad desires, as attested by the fact that sometimes it is translated "lust." The idea is that you have will, or desires, that can go either way—good or bad.

According to the first question of the Westminster Catechism, the chief purpose of human beings is to "glorify God and enjoy him forever." Have you ever considered the possibility that the things you enjoy are the most important things about you? God is serious about your desires, your enjoyment, because the things you enjoy and desire shape every choice you make.

Through the
Eyes of
Your Heart

What do you want? Write down twenty things you want the most. Now answer this: which of those things do you *really* want?

Once you've made your list of things you really, really want, ask yourself another question: what desire or hope or need do you expect those things to fulfill? That's what you really want. How does God meet those needs and desires?

What do you think about the statement that a human being's chief purpose is to glorify God and enjoy him forever? Do you agree that enjoyment is really that important?

Run the Race

Therefore we also, since we are surrounded by so great a cloud of witnesses, let us lay aside every weight, and the sin which so easily ensnares us, and let us run with endurance the race that is set before us, looking unto Jesus, the author and finisher of our faith, who for the joy that was set before Him endured the cross, despising the shame, and has sat down at the right hand of the throne of God.

Hebrews 12:1–2 NKJV

The Big Picture

Hebrews 11 is sometimes called the "Hall of Faith." Here, the anonymous author of Hebrews offers up a list of Old Testament people whose lives demonstrate the truth that it has always been faith, not good works, that pleases God the most. All of these Old Testament believers based their lives on faith in a promise they would never see fulfilled in their lifetimes. They showed incredible strength, they endured incredible hardships, some of them performed incredible miracles, all because they believed that God would do what he said he would do. Every one of those people had enough faith to understand that the things they couldn't see were even more real than the things they could see.

That long list of the faithful in chapter 11 leads right into the practical application in chapter 12. In light of all that faithfulness, "let us lay aside every weight, and the sin which so easily ensnares us, and let us run with endurance the race that is set before us." The point of all those hero stories wasn't to amuse or entertain; it was to inspire. "You can live that way, too!" the writer tells his Hebrew audience. The life of faith is like a race. And if you're running anyway, why not run to win? Get rid of anything that might slow you down. Lay aside the sin. Get serious. Endure. And focus on the prize: Jesus himself, who initiated your faith and will someday perfect it. That's how all those heroes of the faith endured to the end: they focused on the goal. Even Jesus, God made flesh, endured because he was able to focus on what lay ahead for him, not on current difficulties.

You may think of faith as something that exists mostly in the world of ideas. Either you believe in these propositions or you *don't* believe in them. But Hebrews 11 and 12 are about a faith that goes far beyond the bounds of your inner life—a faith that affects everything you do. Why are there even stories to tell about these faithful people? Because they got up and did something about what they believed. And their faith inspires the reader of Hebrews to run to win.

Live by faith until you have faith.

Josh Billings

That phrase "great a cloud of witnesses" is sometimes misunderstood. You're running a race, there are witnesses. You may get the impression that the faith heroes of chapter 11 are the spectators for your race—as if the writer is saying, "A bunch of people are watching, so you'd better run well. You don't want to look like a loser." But that's not what's going on here. That word *witnesses* is rarely used to mean "spectators" in the Bible. It's usually used in a legal sense—people who provide testimony in a court of law. The Old Testament heroes of the faith bear witness to the fact that this race, as difficult as it may be, is worth running.

Look at that first word of chapter 12: "Therefore." It's a pointer back to the previous chapter. It says, in effect, "In light of what you have just heard . . ." In light of all that faithfulness, you can live out a life of faith. You can win the race. And you're going to need that encouragement. The race is tough; it helps to know that others have run this way before. They made it because they kept their eyes on the prize. So can you.

> Someone will say, "You have faith; I have deeds." Show me your faith without deeds, and I will show you my faith by what I do.
>
> James 2:18 NIV

When you're running or biking and you hit a tough hill, your natural reaction is to look down at your feet. Big mistake. When you look down, it seems you're never going to get up the hill. You're focusing on your pain; every step looks exactly like the previous step; it doesn't feel like you're making any progress.

Apply It to Your Life

Everything's different when you lift up your eyes, pick out a mailbox or a street sign at the top of the hill, and focus on that goal. Things seem much more doable. Sure, it still hurts, but you can see the goal getting closer. Quitting no longer seems the only reasonable choice.

Sometimes the going gets hard when you're running the race of faith. You look down at your feet and you don't feel that you're getting anywhere. But if you're going to keep going, you've got to keep looking at Jesus. Lift up your eyes. Forget about how hard it is. Just look up and see the goal: the pleasure of God. You're making more progress than you think you are. Thanks to the great cloud of witnesses who have gone before, the goal seems a lot more doable.

He who lives up to a little faith shall have more faith.
Thomas Brooks

For Hannah Whitall Smith, faith is simple enough—believing God:

"Faith is nothing at all tangible. Faith is simply believing God; and, like sight, it is nothing apart from its object. You might as well shut your eyes and look inside to see whether you have sight, as to look inside to discover if you have faith."

Helen Keller understood the importance of perseverance:

"Be of good cheer. Do not think of today's failures, but of the success that may come tomorrow. You have set yourselves a difficult task, but you will succeed if you persevere; and you will find joy in overcoming obstacles. Remember, no effort that we make to attain something beautiful is ever lost."

Zooming **In**

The Jewish legal system required the word of two witnesses to establish a fact in a court of law. In a death-penalty case, the two witnesses who testified against the defendant had to throw the first two stones at the stoning. The writer of Hebrews provided sixteen witnesses to establish the fact of God's faithfulness!

The heroes listed in the Hall of Faith are Abel, Enoch, Noah, Abraham, Isaac, Jacob, Joseph, Moses, Rahab, Gideon, Barak, Samson, Jephthah, David, Samuel, and the prophets. With the exception of Gideon, Barak, and Jephthah (and some of the prophets), you can read all of these heroes' stories elsewhere in this book.

You have a great cloud of witnesses around you, testifying to the power of faith. And you are a witness yourself. Whether you're thinking about it or not, your life is a testament to the truths of the faith.

Everybody in the Hall of Faith had a story. What's your faith story? What has been memorable about your faith experience?

_____

_____

_____

_____

What are some of the weights and sins that "ensnare" you in your race? How can you throw them off?

_____

_____

_____

_____

When you feel like giving up, how can you keep your eyes on Jesus?

_____

_____

_____

_____

Benji Kelley

Abraham gave up everything he owned and in doing so, acquired everything God had for him.

Do what the LORD wants, and he will give you your heart's desire.

Psalm 37:4 CEV

J. David Hoke

If you really love God with all your heart, soul, mind and strength and want whatever God wants for your life, you can do anything you please because you please to do what God wants you to do and not what God doesn't want for you to do.

The human mind plans the way,
*but the L*ORD *directs the steps.*

Proverbs 16:9 NRSV

John Andrew Holmes

It is well to remember that the entire universe, with one trifling exception, is composed of others.

*Commit yourselves to the L*ORD
and serve him only, and
he will deliver you.

1 Samuel 7:3 NIV

Printed in the United States
By Bookmasters